D0146929

Sep 2016

Mark,

Thank you for commitment to a free, democratic and better Cuba! I hope this book provides a good context for how much was accomplished with greater past freedoms and how much work is needed so that Cuba's future can be much better than its present and its past.

With regards,

Andro

Cuba

From Economic Take-Off to Collapse under Castro

Jorge Salazar-Carillo
and
Andro Nodarse-León

Transaction Publishers

New Brunswick (U.S.A.) and London (U.K.)

Copyright © 2015 by Transaction Publishers, New Brunswick, New Jersey.

All rights reserved under International and Pan-American Copyright Conventions. No part of this book may be reproduced or transmitted in any form or by any means, electronic or mechanical, including photocopy, recording, or any information storage and retrieval system, without prior permission in writing from the publisher. All inquiries should be addressed to Transaction Publishers, 10 Corporate Place South, Suite 102, Piscataway, New Jersey 08854. www.transactionpub.com

This book is printed on acid-free paper that meets the American National Standard for Permanence of Paper for Printed Library Materials.

Library of Congress Catalog Number: 2014040346
ISBN: 978-1-4128-5670-6
eBook: 978-1-4128-5636-2
Printed in the United States of America

Library of Congress Cataloging-in-Publication Data

Salazar-Carrillo, Jorge.
    Cuba : from economic take-off to collapse under Castro / Jorge Salazar-Carrillo, Andro Nodarse-Leon; with a foreword by Alan Heston, a prologue by Robert Z. Aliber, and an introduction by Daniel Murgo.
        pages cm
    Includes bibliographical references and index.
    ISBN 978-1-4128-5670-6
  1. Cuba--History--1933-1959. 2. Cuba--History--1959-1990. 3. Cuba--Economic conditions--1918-1959. 4. Cuba--Economic conditions. 5. Castro, Fidel, 1926---Influence. 6. Communism--Cuba--History. I. Nodarse-Leon, Andro. II. Title.
    F1788.S3144 2015
    972.9106'3--dc23

                                                    2014040346

This book is dedicated to Justo Carrillo Hernández, lawyer, public servant, development banker, and revolutionary, who guided my professional life toward serving Cuba, our fatherland. After many years of researching many other economic topics, I return to the original purpose of my economic studies, which Uncle Justo so fittingly directed.

Jorge Salazar-Carrillo

This book is dedicated to Cuba's future and is a tribute to my family and friends in Cuba, the United States and Spain who have contributed so much to my life over the years. It is specially dedicated to my mother, Miriam Morejón León, and my maternal grandmother, Carmen León Armas, whose unconditional love, guidance, and support formed the core of who I am.

Andro Nodarse-León

Contents

List of Tables

Acknowledgments

We express our debt of gratitude first to Daniel Murgo, PhD, assistant professor of economics at Miami Dade College. Without his untiring care and attention to detail, this book would not have been finished in a timely fashion. He sacrificed many hours in shaping and defining the manuscript while teaching at Florida International University and, in addition to writing an introduction to our book, also contributed to the writing of chapter 7.

Professor Alan Heston, a leading expert on international comparisons at the University of Pennsylvania, propitiated the beginnings of this effort by facilitating our encounter, made very helpful comments at different stages of our work and was was kind enough to write a thoughtful Foreword for our book.

Professor Robert Aliber, a leading expert on financial crises at the University of Chicago, provided useful comments to our work and generously wrote a very insightful and up to date Prologue for our book after his recent visit to Cuba.

A posthumous recognition is also due to Professor Irving Louis Horowitz, who encouraged the preparation of a book that would not only include international comparisons but that would address the economic history of Cuba.

Many thanks are also due to Miriam Morejón León, who was greatly helpful and a source of encouragement during the early days of this project, and to various members of the staff at LEÓN, MAYER & Co. who very capably helped during the last stages of the book.

We are also grateful for the wonderful access to information that we were afforded at the University of Pennsylvania Libraries and the Roberto C. Goizueta Cuban Heritage Collection at the University of Miami, especially to Esperanza de Varona, its long-time director.

Finally, thanks are also due to the Endowment for Cuban American Studies of the Jorge Mas Canosa Freedom Foundation, which kindly provided a grant to support parts of our research and editing.

Jorge Salazar-Carrillo
Andro Nodarse-León

Foreword

Alan Heston

This brief economic history of Cuba from the late nineteenth century to the present day is very timely as relations with Cuba and the United States enter a period of increased interactions. It is fair to say that commentators on Cuban economic development tend to be of two points of view, one that present day Cuba is at a lower economic level than circa 1958, just before the Revolution. A second view cites a number of accomplishments of post-1958 Cuba, while more recently recognizing that there have been a number of failures. It will be clear from the outset that Salazar-Carrillo and Nodarse-León hold the former point of view. In particular, they conclude that the average Cuban is worse off today than in 1958. If Cuba reforms its pricing system and national accounts, it will be possible to get a better understanding of the present level of the Cuban economy.

As background for their case, the authors provide a useful summary of the economic and political developments up to the Revolution. They first bring us through World War II and evolution of Cuba's major international involvement in trade through its sugar industry. Detailed comparisons of the financial sector and real economy take the discussion through the 1950-58 period, their high water mark for Cuba. Like a number of other primary producers, Cuba prospered from the commodity boom associated with the Korean War.

Salazar-Carrillo and Nodarse-León build their case by comparing a substantial number of important economic indicators circa 1958 with some of the same common indicators circa 2010, generally from United Nations sources. While these indicators are usually on a per capita basis, the authors point to wage and consumption indicators to address distributional questions. They make a strong argument that whatever gains in equality that have been obtained in Cuba as a result of egalitarian policies have been accompanied by related economic interventions that have greatly lowered Cuban economic performance compared to its potential. The result, they argue, is that even Cubans at the low end of the income distribution would have had higher incomes today had alternative economic policies been pursued than those followed after the Revolution.

The most common summary measure of per capita GDP is not easily measured in Cuba at present. While there are national currency estimates, there is no easy way to convert them into a basis common with other countries today, or with Cuba in the past. In Cuba in 1958 it is simple enough to convert at exchange rates, and approximations can be done on a purchasing power basis. But not so today because it is a non-market exchange rate; and purchasing power comparisons are difficult because of a multiple pricing system. There is a subsidized price for certain items that are intended to ensure a minimum quantity for all, with other quantities sold at successively higher prices. As a consequence, observers can come to different conclusions about per capita income in Cuba compared to other countries. Cuba was to have fully participated in the 2011 UN-World Bank International Comparison Program but the combination of the fact their national accounts did not meet SNA standards with their non-market prices made it difficult to compare their economic levels with the other 179 countries.

The Report does provide price levels by sector that are derived by linking through other Latin American counties like Peru. However, there is no numerator to go with the denominator so no volume comparisons are made nor is Cuba included in the Latin American totals. It is interesting that the price level index for Cuba is estimated at about 32.2% of the United States, 41.5% of the world average, 42.7% of the 17 Latin American countries and 45.0% of the 22 Caribbean countries. Normally price levels across countries rise with per capita income. On this basis Cuba would be closer to the levels of Bolivia, Nicaragua or Haiti and some distance below Chile, Brazil or Costa Rica.

Based upon their economic indicators, the authors argue that Cuba in 1958 had the physical and human capital that would have permitted substantial economic growth that was stifled by the imposition of controls and nationalization of industries as part of the Revolution. The authors bring to their task experience in the economies of South America and the Caribbean and in the practical issues in economic measurement. Their sources and conclusions are not new but they have succinctly presented their evidence and arguments and made a plausible case that Cuba in 1958 had the resources to be at a materially superior economic level than it is today.

Would Cuba have achieved the level of education and health advances in such a counterfactual economic history? These are not questions on which consensus is easily reached. Hopefully the next decades will permit more study of these issues if more research becomes feasible both individually and jointly on the Cuban economy. Meanwhile, Salazar-Carrillo and Nodarse-León have provided an excellent, if provocative, statement buttressed by empirical support of their assessment that there have been limited improvements, if any, of Cuba's economy during the Castro years.

Alan Heston is a professor emeritus in the Department of Economics at the University of Pennsylvania. He co-directs the University of Pennsylvania's Center for International Comparisons (CIC). Professor Heston is a leading world expert on international economic comparisons and purchasing power parity and is an American Economic Association Distinguished Fellow.

Prologue: The Costs of Arrogance

Robert Z. Aliber

What is the cost of Castro's ego? And who has paid? In 1959, Cuba's per capita GDP was in same ballpark as Spain's. Now per capita GDP in Spain is three to four times higher. Spain has benefited from its integration into Europe and the global economy, while Cuba has been handicapped by its retreat from openness into a largely self-imposed autarchy.

One way to read *Cuba: From Economic Take-Off to Collapse under Castro* is to scan the tables, which are of two types. One type is global standing in terms of per capita GDP, and various other measures of socioeconomic welfare like caloric consumption, TV sets per thousand of population, and longevity, among others. The second type summarizes Cuban production data over the decades: sugar, livestock, tobacco, etc.

Food production has declined because the government has intervened extensively and set prices in various markets to achieve its social goals for health and education and cultural enrichment. The prices in the markets for food and shelter and health care provide little incentive for individuals to save for retirement, and the country's savings rate is so low that there isn't enough money to maintain the capital stock.

Deferred maintenance is readily apparent. Cuba has been "eating" some of the capital that was accumulated in the first half of the twentieth century. Several buildings in Havana crumble every day because of the tropical climate and the lack of maintenance; the rents that are charged to those who live in these buildings are too low to enable whoever owns these properties to provide the repairs so they do not deteriorate. The legions of Chevrolets of the 1950s that dominate the auto fleet were designed when the price of petroleum was $2.00 a barrel; now that the price has reached more than fifty times higher the country doesn't have the money to buy the cars that would be four or five times more fuel efficient.

Cuba was blessed by nature with climate and soils so that it could be a major producer and exporter of tropical fruits. The land gifted by nature to the country is one of the most important components of its capital stock, and yet the contribution that this land might have made to GDP has been stunted because of regulation. The government has set price ceilings on some basic foods; individuals must use ration cards to buy these foods. The prices that farmers receive if they grow more food are too low, and now 40 percent of the land that was once under cultivation is fallow. The land could have been used to grow food for exports, but the prices that the farmers would receive would still be too low, because the price of the Cuban peso is too high. Bushes and shrubs are growing on this land, and a significant investment will have to be made in clearing the land before it can be brought back into cultivation. From time to time, there have been food shortages; the government has been able to figure out how to keep prices low for urban consumers and high enough to keep the individuals producing on the land because it doesn't have enough money to subsidize food consumption without taxing the farmers.

Cuba spends almost 50 percent of the foreign currency that it obtains from its exports of sugar and cigars and tropical fruits and from the gifts from émigrés for imports of foods. Some of these foodstuffs could have been produced at home if the price system, the price of the currency, and the price of foods were not distorted.

The loss of human capital as entrepreneurs and professionals unsympathetic to the government policies have left the country has dampened growth. The government was happy that these groups left, since they were potential members of a political opposition—and their homes and other properties were distributed to its supporters.

The irony is that the annual transfers of money and goods from Cubans in Florida, New Jersey, Spain, and Mexico now are about as large as the country's export earnings. It's a safe bet that the GDP of the two million individuals in the Cuban Diaspora is higher than the GDP of the eleven million individuals that live on the island. Their incomes are high because they have immense capital in terms of their knowledge and skill sets.

The episodic shortages of food, the decrepit quality of the housing stock, and the antique auto fleet suggest that the data that say per capita incomes are $6,000 are misleading. The tragedy of Castro's policies is that they have stunted the country's growth rate; if the rate of GDP growth had been higher by 1.5 percent a year, then GDP today would be twice as high as it now is. The foregone income is a measure of the true cost of one man's ego.

One success of the Castro government is that the literacy rate is among the highest in the world—as it was fifty years ago. The arts flourish. Another success has been medical care; every province has a medical school, and Havana has three. The infant mortality rate and the longevity rate are in the same ballpark as those in the United States. The country exports young doctors under a form of indentureship, comparable in some ways to the service commitment that graduates of West Point and Annapolis and some public health programs have in the United States. Doctors have one of the few skill sets in oversupply. The more effective analogy is with the US farm price support programs, which has led to an oversupply of corn that is sold to foreigners at prices below those in the United States. Cuba is oversupplied with doctors, and some are rented to countries with significantly higher incomes. Many of these individuals would have contributed more to their country's well-being if they had been trained as engineers or agronomists.

Despite the success in reducing infant mortality and increasing longevity, Cuba is dying; its population is shrinking. The suicide rate is among the highest in the world, an increase by a factor of twenty over the last fifty years. Women are "voting with their feet"; the birth rate is 1.7 percent, significantly below the 2.1 percent level required to maintain a constant population. Contraception is freely available—and some women are concerned that food supplies are too uncertain to have children. Moreover, in 2012, 46,000 individuals migrated; most were in the age cohort that would have put them in the active labor force. (A back-of-the-envelope estimate is that there are 150,000 individuals in each one-year age cohort; the implication is that a significant share of individuals in their twenties is leaving.)

The arithmetic is that the increase in the dependency ratio as the more active and the more ambitious of those in the active labor force leave means that living standards for the population will lag behind the increases in other Caribbean countries.

The narrative of *Cuba: From Economic Take-Off to Collapse under Castro* summarizes the various government policies and the consequences of Cuba's go-it-alone stance. Cuba has been afflicted with the economic equivalent of the biblical plagues. The government's belligerence meant that the subsidy implicit in the favored access of sugar to the US market was lost. Then the subsidies from Moscow disappeared when the Soviet Union collapsed. And now the likelihood that the Venezuelan government will continue to provide petroleum at prices much below those of the world market is low. The Cuban leadership has not learned that it is riskier to rely on the goodwill of foreign political leaders than on the market. They will be reminded again when the despot in Caracas reduces the supply of cut-price petroleum because his own economy is on the skids. Imagine the consequences if the Cubans in exile went on strike and stopped their transfers to their relatives for six or ten months.

Castro became the president of Cuba when Dwight Eisenhower was president of the United States; Castro remains in power, or at least he is still around, while there have been ten changes in the US presidency. He has used the police powers of state to maintain his role on the world's political stage, at immense cost to the campesinos that he said he would help. The proportion of the Cuban population that is in jail or prison is higher than in the United States.

The irony is that Castro's ego has had an immensely high cost to the Cuban population as the growth of the economy has been stunted. Some groups are better off, especially those that work for the state. But most are far less well off than if Cuba had continued to grow along with the other countries that have shared in the growing wealth of the global economy. The failure of the Revolution is a useful reminder of the costs of ignoring the price system; those with good intentions forget the law of unintended consequences. US policies that have limited trade, investment, and travel to Cuba have reduced the gains from trade that Cuba might have realized if its own policies had been geared toward greater integration with the global economy. But the cost of these baneful and restrictive US policies has been trivial compared to the costs that the Castro government, with its ignorance and arrogance, has imposed on the population. Eight or ten million Cubans have paid very high costs for some lousy theater.

Robert Z Aliber is professor emeritus of international economics and finance at the Booth School of Business of the University of Chicago. Professor Aliber is a leading world expert in monetary economics and international financial and banking relationships and policy problems. He is the co-author of Manias, Panics, and Crashes, and the author of The New International Money Game, among many other publications.

Introduction

Daniel Murgo

At the end of 1958, Cubans were very hopeful about the future of their country. The end of the Batista dictatorship, the longest dictatorship until that point in Cuba's independent life, was felt as the last obstacle in a process of continuous development. Even though the decade of the 1950s was marked by political restrictions, it was a period of great economic progress. All the economic elements were in place so that, together with a modern democratic system, Cuba could finally secure its place among the most politically and economically developed nations in the world. This book will show how this came to be and how it was ultimately squandered.

The history of Cuba's economic development is covered in twelve chapters. This introduction provides a brief summary of the main findings. The first chapter then presents an overview of the economic history of Cuba until the 1950s. The five that follow provide a detailed portrait of Cuba's economy in the 1950s, just before the Revolution of 1959 brought Communism to the island. These five chapters, with the support of a wide collection of statistics primarily from international organizations, show the place that Cuba had attained among the nations of the world. Chapter 7 analyzes the first stages of the Revolution, especially the abundant legislation and actions that dismantled a market-based economy and replaced it with a centrally planned one. Chapter 8 covers the Cuban economy in detail from the late 1970s to the beginning of the new millennium. Chapter 9 details the structure and collapse of what had been Cuba's largest industry: sugar production. Chapter 10 focuses on the changes to Cuba's economy in the new millennium and chapter 11 provides a synopsis of the country's standing relative to the rest of the world, both in absolute terms and as measured by levels of improvement, after 56 years of Communism. Chapter 12 concludes.

The historical account starts in chapter 1 with Cuba in the first stages of colonial domination. It explains how the port of Havana came to play a key role in the economy of the island. Havana was a hub in the traffic between the colonies and Spain. The existence of cedar forests made the development of the Royal Dockyards of Havana possible. Cuba became the biggest builder of military vessels in America, second only to Spain. Other products like tobacco, leather, beef, and green vegetables were also part of the economy of the island. Sugar was added later, and by the 1820s Cuba had become the richest colony and largest producer of sugar in the world.

The planting, harvesting, transporting, milling, and exporting of sugar cane practically extended all over the island. This meant the importation and adaptation of transport and industrial machinery in Cuba was well ahead of the mother country. Steam boats (1819), railways (1830s), port facilities, telegraphs (1851), warehouses, refineries, modern sugar industrial mills, and others, provided a solid base for the expansion of a modern manufacturing and transportation mentality all over Cuba, which built itself on the shipyard experience that had continued through the earlier centuries. Most of these things happened even though wars of independence were fought from 1868 to 1880 and 1895 to 1898.

The cattle industry, another major pursuit of the landed class in Cuba, was also important, although not as much as the major triumvirate of sugar, tobacco, and coffee. However, prices of internationally traded goods fell between the 1870s and the end of the century, bringing losses to a great number of sugar planters and millers. For Cuba at the end of the nineteenth century the only alternatives to sugar were tobacco and cattle, as the production of coffee had been waning. The only sensible way out of this dilemma was the mechanization that started in the 1880s. That allowed the island to cut costs. It required larger plantations and a new transport alternative based on rails (the price of steel had plummeted as well). United States private foreign investment entered as the main financier of these momentous changes in the productive structure of sugar.

The final and successful War of Independence, known as the Spanish-American War because these two powers were involved, took a toll on both population and economic activity. There was a sharp decrease in the number of sugar mills and the cattle. Horses were severely affected as well.

The two brief American occupations, at the end of the war (1898–1902), and from 1906 to 1909, introduced beneficial economic and political reforms and generally helped the economic recovery of the now independent Cuba. During World War I the role of America in the Cuban economy grew to the point of the United States being the main commercial partner and principal source of investment in the island. By the 1920s the population, decimated in its War of Independence, had recovered and was growing at an average rate of 3.2 percent per year.

The Great Depression deeply affected the economy of Cuba but was partially compensated with public works, and especially by the signing of a Commercial Agreement with the United States in 1934. This last event signaled the start of the economic recovery. By 1959 Cuba had been growing at an average annual rate of close to 10 percent during a period of over twenty years. Cuba's standard of living had risen to a level comparable to that of some Southern states in the United States, which was already at that point, by far, the richest country in the world.

Chapter 2 focuses on Cuba's economic development in relation to the evolution of its real income. The consistently high rates of growth that Cuba experienced since the early 1930s meant that real income almost quadrupled over that time period, leading to greatly improved standards of living. The economy became more diversified as well. This growth was made possible, among other things, by the creation of fundamental economic institutions like the Banco Nacional de Cuba (BNC, Cuba's Central Bank) and the Banco para el Fomento Agrícola e Industrial de Cuba (BANFAIC, Cuba's Development Bank) in the late 1940s and early 1950s. Two well-respected and apolitical professional economists, with abundant international experience, were appointed to run these institutions. As the banking system strengthened, new industries were established, taking advantage of their protection under the GATT Rounds of Annecy (1949) and Torquay (1951). Batista again became president in 1952 through a coup d'état, and political instability increased. However, economic development continued unabated, fueled by both private and public activity. In 1957 Cuba's per capita income was atop Latin America and ahead of a number of European nations, according to United Nations data. Further, UN studies placed Cuba's income per capita among the top third of the world's population. The authors further argue that had the figures been calculated in terms of purchasing power parity, Cuba's relative position would have been even stronger.

Chapter 3 deals with the Cuban currency, prices, inflation, fiscal policy, and international trade. Along with a solid economy, Cuba had a strong currency, a stable fiscal situation, and solid international trade. Three facts characterize the strength of the Cuban peso in the 1950s: (i) the value of the currency per capita was on par with that of the highest income countries; (ii) the value of gold and foreign reserves backing the peso was also high; and (iii) the Cuban peso was a very stable and well-managed currency. For example, currency in circulation per capita was the highest in Latin America, and also higher than West Germany and Denmark, to name a few developed countries, and very close to Austria and Great Britain. This currency was backed by gold and currency reserves that placed Cuba in thirteenth place among countries in per capita terms. Cuban reserves per capita almost doubled those of the UK and nearly tripled those of France. One notable feature is that the strength and stability of the Cuban peso during the republican period happened without any currency control. By the late 1950s Cuba had not experienced a devaluation of its currency in more than twenty years. The value of the peso was almost always on par with the American dollar. Price stability was also a staple of the Cuban economy during its life as an independent nation. Only in years of high inflation the annual rate was close to 3 percent, comparable to US inflation and much lower than countries like Spain, France, Brazil, and Chile. Deflation was never an issue. Fiscal policy was as sound as monetary policy. Cuba exhibited budget surpluses most of the time and only infrequent deficits. The high income per capita and high level of economic development achieved by Cuba also translated into strong international trade. The value of per capita foreign trade was ahead of France and Italy, and even the United States. This was a reflection of an open economy, with a strong and stable currency and comparative advantages in various sectors of its economy. Furthermore, the volume of trade was balanced. Although in general Cuba exhibited trade surpluses most of the time, it exhibited high levels of exports as well as imports.

Chapter 4 analyzes employment, income distribution, and standards of living. As seen in the previous chapters, Cuba in the 1950s was on a path of sustained economic growth. That translated into increasing wages and personal income. The high levels of education, the highly developed financial system and a vibrant business community resulted in full use of the different factors of production. The income generated was, therefore, widely distributed among the sectors of society. The concept of subsistence income, typical of many economies in Latin

America and elsewhere, was alien to Cuba by the end of the 1950s. In terms of compensation to workers as a percentage of GDP, Cuba was close to the most developed countries like the United States and England, and ahead of countries like Switzerland, Australia, and West Germany, to name a few. It was certainly first within Latin America. The labor force participation rate was very high, and very close to that of the United States. Average wages were among the highest in the world. Even though there were minimum wage laws in place, actual wages paid were significantly higher. This was true for the industrial sectors, as well as for agriculture. The unemployment rate was lower than that of the United States and Canada. Sustained economic growth, high levels of employment, and high share of labor income as a percentage of GDP translated into workers of all sectors with high purchasing power. In the consumption of key staples of a rich diet like eggs, sugar, bread, butter, and meat, Cuba was almost always closer to the United States than any other country. Caloric intake was second only to Argentina and Uruguay, two meat-producing countries. This high level of consumption was not restricted to food only. Other indicators like number of cars per capita, number of radio and television stations, and television and radio receivers per capita were the highest in Latin America and sometimes higher than in highly developed Western European countries. The number of movie theaters and newspapers per capita was also very high, indicating a society with not only high income but also a high degree of cultural development.

The same material progress shown in previous chapters also manifested in two other important social indicators: education and health. Chapter 5 addresses these matters. Both private and public sectors made substantial investment in these areas. Economic growth together with advances in education and health care created a virtuous cycle of material growth coupled with social development. Government investment in public education was substantial and was accompanied by an equally strong private sector, typically in the form of religiously affiliated institutions. By 1954 Cuba was spending 4.1 percent of its GDP in education, very close to the United States (4 percent) and ahead of all Western European countries. This made education the second most important item of public expenditure, health care being the first. By 1958, 23 percent of total public expenditure was designated for education, putting Cuba higher than most countries in the world. High expenditure in education translated into high literacy rates, high number of higher education students per one thousand inhabitants, and a high proportion of female students. Complementary measures, like number of libraries per inhabitant, were also among the highest in the world.

Health care was provided by numerous private networks and public hospitals. In 1957 Cuba had more physicians per one thousand habitants than countries like Norway, Sweden, and Great Britain, to name a few. This widely available health care translated into very low total and infant mortality rates. Mortality rate per one thousand habitants was the third lowest in the world, ahead of the Netherlands, Canada, Argentina, and the United States.

All the indicators put together paint a picture of a nation well on the way to sustained economic development. According to Rostow's stages, Cuba was well into the third stage (take-off) and close to the fourth (drive to maturity). This discussion is the subject of chapter 6. Cuba's gross investment as a percentage of GDP was 18 percent in 1957, very close to Sweden (20 percent) and France (19 percent) and ahead of other Western European countries. Even though foreign investment played an important role, domestic investors were taking over key Cuban industries like sugar, agriculture in general, and the financial sector. By 1958, 62 percent of total production of sugar was done by Cuban-owned mills, versus 22 percent in 1939. Simultaneously, US participation in the same sector went from 55 percent in 1939 to 37 percent in 1958. Cuba had a solid infrastructure and high levels of electricity consumption that made production and distribution easier and cheaper. It is also important to stress the significance of the financial sector. In addition to BANFAIC, previously mentioned, other financial institutions like Financiera Nacional and BANDES were created to help different sectors of the economy. At the end of 1958 Cuba was on the way to becoming a highly developed country, closer to the more advance economies in the world than its Latin American neighbors.

Chapter 7 explains how, soon after Fidel Castro came to power in 1959 as part of a broader revolutionary movement to overthrow Batista, Cuba's market-based economy transitioned quickly and violently into a command type of economy. The advent of a Communist regime deprived the country of its more valuable asset: human capital. The socialist policies destroyed the rest of the economy. The quick failure of the first multiannual plan resulted in a rationing system that significantly reduced the consumption level of Cubans. As time went on, the system became more stringent and wider in scope. At the same time a black market developed where prices increased sharply in a short period of time, further worsening the situation of workers.

The collectivization of the agricultural sector introduced a great disruption in production and a sharp decrease in productivity. The traditional organization and production methods were replaced with an inefficient and wasteful planning system that translated into sharp decreases in production and severe damage to cattle and tobacco production.

The progressive collectivization of the economy transformed the government into an overarching monopoly. The incentives present in a market system disappeared, and the remaining private farmers and workers were forced to work more for ever-decreasing compensation.

Sugar, the most important product of the Cuban economy, saw its production and productivity severely diminished. The government was never able to fulfill its promises of increased production. Foreign trade suffered as Cuba found itself oftentimes incapable of fulfilling the target established in its trade agreements with the Soviet Union and its satellite countries.

The worker's compensation and social security systems were adversely affected too. Wages decreased in nominal and real terms, working hours increased, forced labor or "reeducation" was introduced, and the retirement system ceased to be a pay-as-you-go system to become a tool to reward those loyal to the system or punish those who were not.

Finally, the industrialization promised in the early stages of the Revolution never materialized. Cuba ended up playing the sole role of sugar producer in international division of labor in the Communist realm.

Chapter 8 presents a summary of what happened to Cuba from 1972 to 2002. The chapter is divided into four subperiods.

The first subperiod covers from 1972 to 1989. In 1972 Cuba took the important step of becoming a member of CMEA. Prices were set by the government in conjunction with other Communist countries, and international trade was conducted within CMEA and in rubles. This process solidified the role of Cuba as exporter of sugar and, to a lesser degree, nickel and some tropical products. Cuba suffered a chronic trade deficit that had to be compensated with loans, grants, or subsidized import and export prices.

The second subperiod covers from 1989 to 1993. The fall of the Soviet Union signaled the end of the massive subsidies received by Cuba until that point in time. The economic decline was sharp and fast. In a period of five years the economy severely contracted, as seen by its import and export figures.

In the period between 1994 and 1999, also known as "zero option period," the Cuban government undertook substantial reforms to reverse the contraction of the economy that had occurred in 1989–1993. Even though the economy experienced some recovery, especially in the first years, this growth was from the very low levels of 1993–1994. The best estimates is the economy reached, at most, about half of its 1989 level by 1998.

The period of 1999 to 2002 was characterized by a continuation of the reversals seen during the 1994 to 1998 period. The moderate economic liberalizations undertaken during the previous period were reversed, and imports and exports contracted again. Foreign investors were harassed and external creditors held at bay until they retreated from Cuba. Domestic production and investment suffered.

Chapter 9 presents an in-depth look into the evolution of the sugar industry and its decay. When Cuba became a member of CMEA, it was assigned the role of major provider of sugar. Planned increases in production never materialized. However, sugar production required large subsidies of oil and mechanical equipment, and the use of increasingly large areas of land. The production methodology used was highly inefficient and did not take into account the cost of production. With the collapse of the Soviet Union and the end of the subsidies, costs increased substantially and worsened the relative position of Cuba. Concurrently, the world sugar market changed substantially. Brazil became a major exporter, further decreasing the relative importance of Cuba in the world market. Decreases in the price of sugar further reduced the value of Cuban exports.

Chapter 10 analyzes the Cuban economy from 2002 to 2015 and discusses the Cuban government's formulation of new reforms shortly after the transition of power from Fidel to Raul Castro as well as more recent changes that have included the beginning of the normalization of relations between Cuba and the United States.

In chapter 11, a key set of development indicators show the evolution of the Cuban economy vis-à-vis the same group of countries that had been examined in the pre-Castro period. The analysis looks at how these countries rank relative to each other today and measures the rates of improvement achieved by each one over the period since the beginning of the Castro regime. The picture that emerges is a clear one: Cuba's standing after fifty-six years of communism reveals the near total socioeconomic collapse that the country has endured under Castro. The country ranks today among the poorer countries in Latin America across most socioeconomic indicators and is no longer anywhere near the far more advanced peer set that it had before the Revolution. Perhaps surprisingly, the authors are also able to show that, with respect to the two social indicators so often touted by the Castro regime as areas of exceptional achievement for Cuba, namely education and health care, the real picture is far more nuanced. For example, while Cuba's standing on basic measures of literacy is among the highest in the world today, many other countries have been able to replicate such improvements in literacy over the same time period. Furthermore, education, more broadly, is severely hampered in Cuba by the government's heavy censorship of entire schools of thought. Similarly, with respect to health care, the authors highlight that Cuba's improvement with respect to infant mortality and other metrics is not unique to Cuba, as many other countries have actually achieved greater improvements in those metrics than Cuba has over the same time period. In fact, Cuba's ranking with respect to infant mortality has actually fallen within the sample set that was evaluated for the pre-Castro period. Furthermore, when one looks beyond basic statistics, one finds a health care system that is plagued by shortages of basic medicines and a lack of advanced equipment and treatment technologies.

In the final chapter, the authors succinctly summarize their findings and draw important conclusions about how a country's developmental progress alone cannot shield it from ruinous political experimentation. Importantly, the authors also stress that the success of the Cuban republic up until the end 1958 can be a source encouragement for capital markets to invest in the reconstruction of Cuba once the appropriate legal and political frameworks have been put into place and, simultaneously, serve as inspiration for Cubans to draw from when they have an opportunity to rebuild the nation on a new foundation of liberty and individual initiative.

1

The Economic History of Cuba before 1950

Cubans are very proud of their country's achievements as a free republic. This pride has sometimes led to lively exchanges among academics and professionals on the matter of why Cuba was in fact so distinguished among nations. One such exchange famously occurred in Washington, DC, between Felipe Pazos, first president of the Cuban central bank (Banco Nacional de Cuba) and the Englishman Philip Glaessner, whose PhD dissertation at Harvard was the cornerstone of perhaps the most famous book on the economics of the island at the time: Henry Wallich's *Monetary Problems of an Export Economy: The Cuban Experience 1914–1947.*[1] In a debate between Glaessner and Pazos on the drivers of Cuba's economic development, Glaessner went on and offered up a long list of intricate postulates to explain the island's economic progress. As Glaesner finished, Pazos, who had been waiting to get in a word, quickly took the Englishman off of his pulpit with a quick punchline: Cuba's developmental success, Pazos stated, was simply the result of it benefiting from the mysterious blessing of being a large island proximate to a prosperous continent. Quickly connecting Pazos's comments to his own home country (the UK), Glaessner had no choice but to reply, "Ah, so true, so true."

The mystery of Cuba's economic development really started with the Indian population, so different from those of the rest of the Caribbean and the northern part of South America. The tainos and siboneyes that originally populated the island were sedentary, as opposed to the caribes, who dominated, by incursions and force, the rest of the territory and who were hunter-gatherers. Thus, Cuban primitive societies were more advanced. At the same time, however, the population of the island at the end of the fifteenth century was sparse, which facilitated the conquest by the Spaniards at that juncture. By 1510 the circumnavigation and conquest of Cuba had been accomplished and the first

1

capital established in Baracoa (1511), its most eastward city, and very close geographically to Hispaniola (today the Dominican Republic and Haiti), which had been the initial choice of Columbus, but which was much smaller and was populated by fierce Indians. By the time the conqueror Diego Velázquez (under orders by Diego Colón, the governor of Hispaniola) became the first captain general of Cuba, the capital had been established in the most guarded and promising harbor city of Santiago de Cuba, from where Hernán Cortés, who had aided the former in the conquest of Cuba, was sent to Veracruz for the eventual conquest of Mexico.

The premier position of Cuba strengthened further when the city of Havana was founded in its northwestern coast, almost diagonally opposite to Santiago de Cuba, beginning in 1514, finally settling where it now stands in the year 1519. The city became such an important military and naval hub that it was dubbed "the key to the New World" very early after its inception. This was officially recognized by Regent Queen Maria Ana of Spain in 1665, when Havana's coat of arms was approved to include a key in its design.[2] It was also from Havana that the expeditions of Cuban Governor and Commander of Florida Hernando de Soto originated into what is now the United States of America. Within less than a half-century later the similar expeditions of Pedro Menéndez de Avilés left from Havana as well.

As a result of the importance of Havana, and its close relation to Florida, it was continuously embattled by pirates, corsairs, and filibusters of British, French, and Dutch origins seeking to capture treasures from Spanish galleons. At the time, the routes for the Spanish Royal Fleets, which operated from and to the port of Cádiz in Southwestern Spain, branched into three as they approached Caribbean waters. One went to Cartagena in present-day Colombia, another to Portobelo in present-day Panamá, and the third to Veracruz, in Nueva España (New Spain), a vice-royalty, and presently Mexico. There they delivered foodstuffs and manufactured products from the mother country[3] and loaded up with gold and spices in the former ports, and spices and silver in the latter. With that precious cargo onboard they converged in Havana, to jointly undertake the return voyage. Because of that important convergence, in addition to the attractiveness that it already presented to the buccaneers and naval agents of the contesting sea powers, Havana became fortified with three stupendous fortresses, abundant garrisons, and provisions, and the berthing of armed ships.

To understand the situation fully, and Havana as its centerpiece, it should be explained that the Spanish Royal Fleet returned to Spain with its precious cargo using the force of the Gulf Stream that passes north of Havana and borders the east coast of Florida up to St. Augustine, sharply swerving toward Europe at this point. Therefore, it was essential for the Spaniards to control activities in Florida, and so they did from the vantage of Havana, to the oldest American city of St. Augustine and its strategic fortifications along the Matanzas inlet (Fort Matanzas) and the castle fronting the city and bay (Castillo de San Marcos).[4]

All this explains the importance that early on was attained by Havana as a hub and *entrepôt*. As agriculture, commerce, and industry prospered, Havana's government became the centerpiece of the Spanish colonies in the Americas, tying together, through seafaring lanes, the Vice-Royalty of Nueva España (Mexico), the Capitanía General de Guatemala (Central America) and the Province of Nueva Granada (Colombia, Ecuador, and Venezuela, including Panamá). One additional important factor that allowed Havana to gain even greater strategic importance, and also served as an important driver of urban expansion throughout the island beyond the seven cities (really villages in terms of today's populations) originally founded by Velázquez, was the fact that Cuba was large and had abundant forests with high-quality wood. Cuban cedar was reputedly the best for battleships, and forestry became the basis for shipbuilding in what became the Royal Dockyards of Havana.[5] As a result, Havana and Cuba became the biggest builder of military vessels in America, ranking as equal to the Spanish navy yards in Galicia and Vizcaya. This continued until the late 1700s, creating an abundant supply of carpenters, caulkers, and blacksmiths[6] and turned Havana into "an unparalleled maritime city"[7] during the sixteenth, seventeenth, and eighteenth centuries and "an important military and naval hub"[8] known as the Royal Arsenal of the Navy, or alternatively the Royal Dockyard of Our Lady of Bethlehem. In the eighteenth century well over 30 percent of all the ships of the Spanish Navy were built at Havana.[9] Although tourism was an insignificant part of the international exchange of goods and services at the time, the fact is that the Havana dockyards represented a tourist attraction, particularly during the launch or the careening of a ship at the Arsenal.[10] This constituted an additional contribution to the strength of the Cuban economy during these centuries. After the British invaded and controlled Cuba in 1762, the novel yard had to be rebuilt when they left in 1763. This required four thousand laborers and substantial funding, being completed only by 1765. That year Havana was declared "primary port and naval station."[11] The "renewed yard boasted four levels of tiers, one shipway for small vessels, two piers, a set of tackle blocks, a factory to make sails and a rigging loft, warehouses, a foundry, forges, hydraulic saw, a hospital, a prison gallery, a cemetery, the residential quarters of the commanding general, and many other facilities.[12] Its length was over one kilometer. The dockyard began to decline at the beginning of the nineteenth century, but it was still active until the 1890s, although the *Colón*, the last ship built there, was launched in 1852.[13]

It should be understood that Havana represented during this period about 40 percent of the population of Cuba. In fact, the census of 1794 calculated it as 44 percent. It was a purveyor of food, beef, green vegetables, and fruit for Spain.[14] The city was also where tobacco was first cultivated, mostly destined for the city of Seville, the principal consumption point in Europe. Cattle ranching was the other important activity, which vied with the tobacco growers for the governance of the Spanish colony. As tobacco production doubled during the eighteenth century, even the ranchers became involved in what became the principal export product of the island, and its most profitable and famous (and indigenous) plant. The ranchers in turn were still actively exporting leather and beef, directly or indirectly (through the treasure fleets) to Spain.[15] The sailors consumed basically jerked or dried beef during their voyages.

But at the end of the eighteenth century something new and different was brewing in Cuba that would justify the saying of Abbé Raynal: "The Island of Cuba alone might be worth a kingdom to Spain." This had to do with sugar and its rapid expansion. So profound an influence it had over the island that "in the late 1820s Cuba had become the richest colony and the largest sugar producer in the world,"[16] with the United States as its main trading partner despite Spanish tariffs. This was greatly aided by the demise of sugar production with the independence of Saint Domingue (soon called Haiti). Saint Domingue's production of sugar had declined by almost one third between 1791 and 1802, and to practically nothing by 1825. Production significantly declined as well in Jamaica. As a result, the price of the sweet increased twofold between 1788 and 1795. And finally, many of the planters from the old Saint Domingue established themselves in and brought their sugar producing practices to the easternmost territory of Cuba.

Yet it has to be recognized that fertile grounds for this expansion had been prepared by the technology-minded creoles in Cuba, led by the

Sociedad Económica de Amigos del País. The leader of the Sociedad, Arango y Parreño, brought the first steam-powered mill to Cuba in 1794 from Europe, although its application was not completely successful. But where this experiment failed, water wheels proved to be a success. As a result of the expansion of sugar, controlled mostly by the merchant and commercial classes, roads were built to cut transport costs to the port of Havana. Production spread throughout the island, spurred by the high sugar prices of the 1790s, and it seemed that "the Cubans now almost had the world sugar market in their hands."[17] After the Napoleonic Wars the production of sugar[18] increased greatly, together with that of tobacco and coffee, which diversified still more the fundamental activities of the island. But most importantly, in 1818 the North American market was legally opened for the Cuban merchants.[19]

As the century moved on, the "wealth of Cuba between 1825 and the end of the nineteenth century grew to first-class levels."[20] It depended in part on the newly attained importance of coffee until 1840, but overwhelmingly on sugar. Havana was its most important center of population, which according to the 1827 census reached 112,000 inhabitants, this made Havana larger than any city in the United States, with the exception of New York City, which in the 1820 census had a population of 123,706 inhabitants. In the countryside the sugar plantation experienced a complete improvement in technology, mostly on the industrial side, (the first sugar mill steam engine was introduced in 1794), attaining the form common in the twentieth century. The plantations expanded well outside the capital, based on extensive farming of cane, having as a consequence the "destruction of the great mahogany and cedar trees of Cuba begun by the navy and the builders of the Escorial."[21] The extension of planting, harvesting, transporting, milling and exporting of sugar cane all over the island led to levels of importation and adaptation of transport and industrial machinery that were well ahead of the mother country. Steamboats (1819), railways (1830s), port facilities, telegraphs (1851), warehouses, refineries, and modern sugar industrial mills provided a solid base for the expansion of a modern manufacturing and transportation mentality all over Cuba, which built itself on the shipyard experience that had continued from earlier centuries.[22]

Many would probably question how all this could be possible given the Cuban Wars of Independence during the last third of the nineteenth century between the islanders and the Spaniards in the "ever faithful Island of Cuba," as they used to say in Spain. The Ten Years' War that started late in 1868 was mostly confined to the Eastern province, mostly Puerto Príncipe (Camagüey) and Oriente. These were vast expanses where the cattle industry, another major pursuit of the landed class in Cuba (although not as important as the major triumvirate of sugar, tobacco, and coffee referred to above) was predominant. Sugar being relatively unimportant there, it is not surprising that the record harvest ending in June 1868 of 750,000 tons (double the production in the 1850–54 quinquennium) was almost matched by the 725,000 tons of 1869, which was almost equal to the harvest of 1870 (by then Cuba produced 42 percent of the world's sugar supply), while a new record of 775,000 tons was set in 1873. Even after the Western invasion staged by General Máximo Gómez in 1874 burned eighty-three plantations in Sancti Spiritus and Cienfuegos, just southwest of Camagüey, the 1875 harvest came in well over 700,000 tons. But the next three years felt the impact of the war in that region and in Oriente in terms of sugar production, although the crop recovered in 1879.

However, although the Ten Years' War and the much smaller Guerra Chiquita did not significantly affect what was now King Sugar in the island, the early 1880s saw a retrenchment to levels that had been achieved twenty years earlier (the 1880–84 mean production was 527,400 tons per year), which was partly recouped in 1885–90 by an increase of over 150,000 tons per year over the previously mentioned five year average.[23] But there was a quick recovery in the 1890s, with bumper crops exceeding 900,000 tons yearly from 1891–1895, with the last year attaining a million tons for the first time.

What was behind the success in the last decade of the nineteenth century? With the end of the slave trade the merchants saw their finances deteriorate, which had been the wherewithal for the planters, although at high interest rates (over 20 percent per year frequently would be charged). But this was partially explained by the legal prohibition of encumbering the mills to pay for debts. But a new mortgage law introduced in the 1880s made this possible, adding land as well (before, only the crops could be attached). This brought forth a lowering of the interest rates for the harvesting and milling of sugar.

Additionally, prices of internationally traded goods fell between the 1870s to the end of the century, bringing losses to a great number of sugar planters and millers. For Cuba at the end of the nineteenth century the only alternatives to sugar were tobacco and cattle, as the production of coffee had been waning. The only sensible way out of this dilemma was the mechanization started in the 1880s; that would allow the island to cut costs. This required larger plantations and a new transport alternative based on rails (the price of steel had plummeted as well). US private foreign investment entered as the main financier of these momentous changes in the productive structure of sugar. These funds were applied to the coming together of several plantations into a central one (thus the name "central," in Spanish, for the sugar mills), which ground their cane and was linked to them by rail. Most of the planters were tenants. Others were landowners that raised sugar cane to be milled in the sugar mills. These arrangements led to the creation of "colonatos," with the "colonos" receiving a share of the proceeds from the sale of the raw sugar by the sugar mills, based on the weight ("arrobaje") of the cane provided to the "centrales." "Indeed the more the matter is examined the more it seems that this revolution of the 1880s, as it is often regarded, was the most important social change that the island of Cuba has experienced; for it was then that Cuba lost her old upper-class based on land, so that, alone among the South American states, she would later embark on independence with her social revolution already accomplished."[24]

The War of Independence turned this panorama upside down. The havoc created by this war to the death that the Spaniards promised to fight, according to the Conservative Prime Minister of Spain Antonio Cánovas del Castillo "to the last peseta and the last drop of blood" destroyed Cuba.[25] The impact of the over three-year conflagration was such that it can be measured in population losses and economic declines. Taking the former one first, the 1899 census counted 1,572,845 inhabitants. In 1895, this figure had been approximately 1,800,000.[26] In terms of production acreage used for cultivation, it declined over 30 percent during the War of Independence, half of it devoted to sugar cane. Of the 1,100 sugar mills in 1894, only about 200 were worth saving. In fact only 168 mills ground sugar in 1901.[27] The census undertaken by the American occupying forces in 1899 gave proof of the slaughter of cattle during the previous conflagration. When compared with the 1894 statistics, only one out of every six horses and one of eight heads of cattle remained standing. Yet Havana, with a population of about 240,000, "was still one of the great cities of America,"[28] in contrast to many small towns that had been destroyed, as well as their links. However, the Treaty of Paris, signed at the end of the war, had the favorable result of eliminating all of the foreign debt of the former colony.

During the occupational interregnum between 1899 and 1902, the American government in Cuba achieved substantial improvements in the economic conditions in the island, principally in the areas of education and sanitation. Other achievements of particular importance for the economic well-being of Cuba were the construction of the Central Railroad, which linked the eastern provinces with Havana; the building of hundreds of miles of highways with the required bridges; the establishment of over three thousand miles of telephonic and telegraphic lines; the almost tripling of the production of sugar between 1899 and 1902, which led to an increase in the value of Cuban exports of almost 100 percent between those years; and an expansion of the population by just over two hundred thousand inhabitants.[29] Still, the recovery of the economy to the peak attained in 1894–1895 was still a long way from being achieved.

On May 20, 1902, Cuban Independence Day, the island's economy was badly damaged, with agricultural production having gone down to a small fraction of its 1894 level. The War of Liberation from Spain had taken its toll. Yet, the First American Intervention had initiated a clear economic recovery.[30]

Tomas Estrada Palma, as the independent republic's first president, decided to organize the economy following conservative ideas. Therefore, Estrada Palma's administration relied on the legal codes and methods of the colonial epoch, which tended to be rather inflexible. At the same time, President Estrada Palma prioritized relations with the United States. In 1902 a Commercial Reciprocity Treaty was signed with the United States. In addition, Estrada Palma obtained an American debenture loan for $35 million, at the time a relatively large figure, which expressed confidence in the Cuban nation.

Cuba's economy quickly returned to intense sugar exploitation to satisfy a growing export market. The devastated rural economy continued recovering through the construction of roads and highways, financed principally by the rise of sugar production. The Second American Intervention of 1906 drew up various fundamental laws, such as that establishing the Civil Service, which constructed eight hundred kilometers of highways and two hundred bridges, and expanded public health care. The government's main source of tax collections continued to be customs duties. In 1909 the second elected president, José Miguel Gómez, took over. With the treasury short of funds, an international loan was arranged to cover a deficit of $9 million. During this period, innovations in sugar agronomy were introduced, which supported its continued expansion. The economy had a clear neoclassical bent, with a firm belief in international specialization and free enterprise.

Cuba's exports, which had been $64 million in 1902, rose to $151 million in 1910. Sugar production rose from 300,000 Spanish long tons in 1900 to 1,843,000 in 1910. With incredible speed, Cuba had more than recovered economically from the War of Independence.

Mario Garcia Menocal, Cuba's third president, was elected to begin his term in 1913. A small international debenture loan for $10 million was contracted, and Cuban money was issued for the first time in 1914, governed by the gold standard. However, the issuance of paper money was not undertaken, with American currency being the principal means of payment. Menocal was reelected and carried out the census of 1919, which counted 2,889,004 persons, an increase of more than 80 percent in twenty years. This growth was one of the fastest in the world in those years, equivalent to a 3.2 cumulative annual percentage rate. Exports were $575 million that year, almost four times those of 1910, when overall consumer prices, measured by the United States Historic Consumer Price Index, less than doubled.[31] Sugar production reached four million metric tons, more than doubling production in fewer than ten years. These and other factors led to a remarkable financial deepening in the Cuban economy, with the Havana Bourse achieving the highest ratio of market capitalization to GDP in the world.[32] In an article by Christopher Gray appearing in the New York Times Mr. Gray writes: "At the beginning of the twentieth century, the Cuban capital was spectacularly rich, Newport-rich, . . . in the early twentieth century the section around Obispo and O'Reilly was home to so much bank construction it was nicknamed little Wall Street."[33]

The First World War brought stratospheric sugar prices, especially during the postwar era, and the so-called Dance of the Millions in Cuba. With the average cost of production at one cent per pound, sugar came to be sold for more than twenty-two cents, and its exports reached almost one billion dollars in 1920. At today's prices these figures would be more than nine times those indicated, making the island perhaps the richest country per capita in the world in that year.

The bubble burst at the end of that very year, when Cuba, then the largest sugar producer and exporter in the world, overproduced and could only find buyers at about four cents per pound. The Cuban land-owners lost their properties because they could not pay back the loans arranged during the boom. A similar tragedy occurred with Cuban banking. Lacking capital to deal with its losses, due to the multiple bankruptcies of national companies, and suffering a grave liquidity crisis, the banking industry had, with a few exceptions, to terminate its operations. The beneficiaries of this debacle were the foreign sugar companies, especially the American ones, which ended up controlling a good part of the sugar industry and agricultural production in the nation. Even more extreme was the already noted disappearance of the Cuban banks, which were practically reduced to a bare minimum; while those of Yankee nationality came to control the bulk of the banking deposits and assets, whereas before the former represented around 70 percent of the total.

In 1921 Alfredo Zayas y Alfonso began his term in office, as well as the process of recovery of the Cuban economy, with the consolidation of the country's debt. Public spending decreased, and fiscal revenue increased through taxes on the wealthy classes. Agricultural diversification was supported by the new lending-for-production law (*Ley de Refacción*), which facilitated the expansion of production both of sugar and other crops.

In 1925 Gerardo Machado inaugurated his government. The situation in the sugar markets was characterized by overproduction. Yearly production in Cuba, which was somewhat more than 20 percent of the world's total, expanded to 5,189,347 Spanish long tons in that year (equivalent to 5,345,028 in today's metric ton measurements). Beginning in 1927, no new sugar mills were built in Cuba, and production started to decrease. The crisis in the country's main industry brought with it an economic slump and a serious increase in unemployment in the nation, which still was one of the richest countries in the world per head of population.

To compensate, a series of public construction projects were carried out, financed by international loans, with the central highway being their axis, particularly with regards to their economic impact. The protective tariffs of 1927 were also introduced, aimed at promoting domestic industry. Machado's second term began in 1929. The winds of the Great Depression began to be felt with the collapse of the New York Stock Exchange in October of that year. Foreign investment turned negative that year, which had not happened since 1919, and immigration practically stopped. In the subsequent years, although the central highway was finished in 1931,[34] public finances weakened, and from 1931 to 1933 the population of the country contracted due to emigration off of a peak of 3,962,344 inhabitants counted in 1931.

After touching bottom in 1932–33, Cuba's economy began to recover in 1934 with the signing of a Commercial Agreement with the United States (the first signed by the United States of many to follow).

The political illegality and instability initiated by Machado with his 1929 extension of power (Prórroga) seemed to begin to come to an end in 1936, but the process stagnated and extended until 1940. However, Cuban exports recovered by about 50 percent between 1933 and 1940, together with the production of sugar. World commerce, which had fallen to 10 percent of its value during the greatest economic crisis of the contemporary world, began to recover with the multiple bilateral agreements initiated by the Americans, who had been motivated to act by the fall of their gross national product to 50 percent of its potential, and an unemployment rate of 25 percent.

The Cuban Constitution of 1940 restored political order. It also instituted basic economic changes in society. Batista was elected president that year. With the Second World War, the volume of exports and the price of the principal Cuban crops at that time (coffee, tobacco, and sugar) increased, with the agricultural mechanization of the latter now increasingly possible. Cuba became the main sugar supplier of the Allies through the United States, to which it sold its entire harvest at controlled prices, given the rationing and price ceilings established for foodstuffs in most of the world. It received in exchange a debenture loan from the American government for $25 million to carry out construction and absorb unemployed labor. After that loan another followed for $11 million to finance sugar production during the war, as well as various lend-lease agreements. Under the direction of Carlos Hevia, Cuba's Office of Regulation of Prices and Supplies (ORPA) stimulated the creation of war industries to take advantage of the scarcities created by WWII and drive further economic growth on the island. During this episode the foreign exchange value of the Cuban peso stood at a significant premium to the US dollar, at one time surpassing $1.17 per peso.

In 1944 Ramón Grau San Martin entered into power, and during the postwar period the prices of sugar shot up, representing great increases in Cuba's export values. This bonanza made possible a broad plan of public construction and school improvements. In 1947 exports were over two and a half times those of 1941, with sugar production surpassing the previous record of 1925.

Notes

1. Wallich, Henry C. *Monetary Problems of an Export Economy: The Cuban Experience 1917–1947.* Cambridge: Harvard University Press, 1950.
2. Later he sent Pánfilo Narvaez, famous for exterminating over one hundred thousand Indians in the Western territory that became known as Matanzas

(killings), to force Cortes to return to Cuba—and the rest, with the burning of his ships, is part of the history of Mexico.

3. In fact, later on the whole of Cuba was given the term of key to the Gulf (of Mexico), which cannot only be understood by its role in the history, society, and economics of this expanse, but is clearly understood if the geography of the area is considered.

4. Pedro Menéndez de Avilés founded the city in 1565, fifty-three years after Florida was discovered by Ponce de León. It attracted the attention of the most famous corsair of the sixteenth century, Sir Francis Drake, which raided the city prompting the building of a stronger castle (San Marcos), after which St. Augustine became inexpugnable. All these activities were controlled from Havana.

5. Zúñiga, Antonio Ramos. "The Royal Dockyard of Havana." *Herencia* 15.3 (2009).

6. An interesting fact is that with Pedro Menéndez de Avilés being the governor of Cuba in 1568, six small galleons were built in Havana, whose qualities were considered equal to those built in Vizcaya, but moreover constituted innovative prototypes of the frigates of the eighteenth century and the clippers of the next century. *Ibid.*, pg. 23.

7. *Ibid.*, pg. 22. Also, consult: Luna, Félix. *Breve Historia de los Argentinos.* Bueno Aires: Grupo Editorial Planeta, 2000. Pg. 17–18.

8. Ibid., pg. 22.

9. Harbron, John D. *Trafalgar and the Spanish Navy.* London: Conway Maritime Press, 1988. Pg. 15.

10. Zúñiga, op. cit., pg. 25.

11. Ibid., pg. 25.

12. Ibid., pg. 27.

13. Ibid., pg. 27.

14. Thomas, Hugh. *Cuba: The Pursuit of Freedom.* New York: Harper & Row, 1971.

15. "Hides were Cuba's main export till the eighteenth century tobacco boom." Ibid., pg. 24.

16. Ibid., pg. 61.

17. Ibid., pg. 80.

18. Thanks to Haitian exiles and government support, coffee exports went from 80 tons in 1792 to 12,000 tons in 1823 and continued at more or less those levels till 1844. Tobacco expanded rapidly as well till 1850, when 350 million cigars were exported, before the 1857 tariff.

19. In addition, the productivity of agricultural production increased over 50 percent from 1790, as a result of better technology.

20. Ibid., pg. 109. By the 1870s Cuba produced 42% of the world's sugar.

21. Ibid., pg. 119.

22. The riches in Cuban production translated as well into high consumption standards, as indicated by the following quote: "each Cuban probably consumed $80 (£18) a year per head of foreign produce—an amazing figure for the nineteenth century." Ibid., pg. 125.

23. The yearly average production of the six years in question was 647,000 tons. The 1865–1875 mean production of sugar was 676,000 tons. The increasing production of sugar from beets in Europe after a technological discovery there was the main reason for this decline.

24. Ibid., pg. 278.
25. From his formal speech in March 23, 1895, upon assuming power. See: Tone, John Lawrence. *War and Genocide in Cuba, 1895–1989*. Chapel Hill: University North Carolina Press, 2006. Pg. 49.
26. Thomas, op. cit., pg. 423.
27. Ibid., *pg. 428. Tobacco also contracted but only by about 18%.*
28. Ibid., pg. 433.
29. Cuban Economic Research Project, University of Miami. *A Study on Cuba*. Coral Gables: University of Miami Press, 1965.
30. For reference on this section of the chapter *c.f.*: Salazar-Carrillo, Jorge. "One Hundred Years of Cuban Economy." *Herencia*. 8.1–2. Pg. 16–23.
31. *Historic Consumer Price Index 1800–1998*. Ann Arbor: University of Michigan Documents Center, 2003. Pg. 1–3.
32. Rajan, Raghuram G. and Zingales, Luigi. "The Great Reversals: the Politics of Financial Development in the 20th. Century". Journal of Financial Economics 69 (2003) 5–50.
33. Gray, Christopher. "Havana's New York Accent." New York Times, 15 Mar 2012.
34. Collegium of Cuban Economists. *The Cuban Economy Past, Present and Future*. Coral Gables: Collegium of Cuban Economists, 1997. Additionally, see: Cuban Economic Research Project, University of Miami. *A Study on Cuba*. Op. cit. Also, see: Cuban Economic Research Project. *Stages and Problems of Industrial Development in Cuba*. Coral Gables: University of Miami Press, 1965.

2

Economic Development and National Income in the 1950s

As the 1950s began, Cuba had a lot to be proud of with respect to the level of economic development it had achieved in its brief history as a free republic. The decade of the 1950s ushered in further advances in the diversification of the Cuban economy, the creation of additional institutions to support ongoing economic development, ongoing growth of the country's middle class, and continuous improvement in the island's measures of living standards.

Carlos Prio Socarras was elected president in 1948, and his term was characterized by the strengthening of the national and developmental banking systems with the creation of the Banco Nacional de Cuba (BNC), (the Cuban central bank) in December of 1948 and, in December of 1950, the creation of the Banco para el Fomento Agrícola e Industrial de Cuba (BANFAIC), (the development Bank of Cuba). At the same time, new industries were established through the advantages that Cuba was able to gain in the GATT (General Agreement on Tariffs and Trade) negotiations of Annecy and Torquay, led by the newly created Department of Economic Affairs of the Cuban Ministry of State (Foreign Affairs). Well-respected apolitical figures were put in charge of these institutions, which were properly intertwined to collaborate. Felipe Pazos, a well-respected economist trained at Columbia University who had been a member of the Cuban delegation to the 1944 Bretton Woods Conference and had subsequently been part of the staff of the International Monetary Fund during the late 1940s, was the founding president of the BNC. Justo Carrillo, also a well-respected economist, who had led the Cuban delegation to the GATT negotiations and had directed the just-mentioned Department of Economic Affairs, was made president of the BANFAIC, and acted as ex-officio vice president of the BNC.

The three-year period of 1951–53 witnessed annual sugar production levels that were new records for the island (7,225,475 metric tons in 1952) as well as the second-highest total exports ($766 million in 1951). By 1953, Cuba's population had reached 5,829,029, as registered by that year's census, representing an increase of almost 50 percent since 1931.

On March 10, 1952, as Prio's term was coming to an end, Batista became president of Cuba again, but this time as a result of a coup d'état under the pretext that the upcoming elections were going to be rigged. Batista's return to power via force was viewed with distaste by many within Cuba, and political instability and dissatisfaction grew among the Cuban people. Eventually, this dissatisfaction led various political movements to organize, with significant popular support, to remove Batista and reinstate the democratic and institutional processes prescribed by the Constitution of 1940. Despite a level of political turmoil that would have halted the growth of many other countries, the developmental momentum in Cuba's economy was such that economic progress continued throughout the 1950s, fueled by both private and public sector activities — including a great deal of construction activity and expansion of the financial sector, with the latter in turn helping to finance further expansions in agricultural activity and more diversified growth in industrial production.

After Cuba suffered through a period of depression from 1932 to 1933, its gross national product grew at an average rate of close to 10 percent annually for over twenty years, with the island's national income almost quadrupling on a real basis between the early 1930s and 1958. As table 1 shows, by 1957 Cuba's per capita income was among the very top in Latin America[1] and, even more impressively, surpassed or was similar to that of a number of countries in Western Europe and Asia, which are today some of the world's most advanced economies. Cuba's per capita income, for example, was only 7 percent lower than Italy's, 20 percent higher than Spain's, 33 percent higher than Greece's and nearly double Portugal's. Additionally, Cuba's per capita income was 50 percent higher than Japan's, which was then, as it is now, the most developed country in Asia.

A study published by the United Nations in 1950, encompassing seventy countries that together accounted for 90 percent of the world population and over 90 percent of the world's total income showed similar results, captured in table 2, where Cuba's GDP per capita as of that time placed the country's population in the top third of world population in terms of income.

Table 1. GDP per Capita in 1957.

Country	GDP Per Capita (in USD)	Country	GDP Per Capita (in USD)
United States	2,141	Spain	315
Sweden	1,276	Lebanon	312
Switzerland	1,224	Greece	286
New Zealand	1,170	Costa Rica	274
Australia	1,074	Argentina	256
Luxembourg	1,070	Japan	249
United Kingdom	957	Dominican Republic	239
Belgium	917	Mexico	234
Norway	914	Portugal	199
France	855	Philippines	194
West Germany	742	Honduras	166
Netherlands	697	Guatemala	160
Finland	651	Brazil	156
Austria	541	Ecuador	150
Ireland	445	Colombia	147
Italy	407	Thailand	98
Cuba	**379**	Paraguay	85
Union of South Africa	349	India	61
Yugoslavia	339	Pakistan	52
Panama	327	Burma	47

Source: GDP figures are from: Statistical Office of the United Nations, Department of Economic and Social Affairs. *Statistical Yearbook 1959.* New York: Statistical Office of the United Nations, 1959. Pg. 447–448. The GDP per capita for Uruguay is from: Statistical Office of the United Nations, Department of Economic and Social Affairs. *Monthly Bulletin of Statistics.* New York: Statistical Office of the United Nations, 1961. The population data utilized to convert GDP figures to per capita figures are from: Statistical Office of the United Nations, Department of Economic and Social Affairs. *Demographic Yearbook 1958.* New York: Statistical Office of the United Nations, 1958. Pg. 110–121 for all countries except Cuba, which had more recent data in: Banco Nacional de Cuba. *Memoria 1958–59.* Havana: Banco Nacional de Cuba, 1959. 95. Pg 95. Figures were converted from national currency to USD based on the exchange rates published in Statistical Office of the United Nations, Department of Economic and Social Affairs. *Statistical Yearbook 1957.* New York: Statistical Office of the United Nations, 1957. Pg. 944.

Table 2. Distribution of World Income in 1950.

Per Capita GDP Range (USD)	% of World Population	% World Wealth Held	Representative Countries	GDP Per Capita (USD)
420–1,453	15%	62%	United States	1,453
			Canada	870
			Sweden	780
			UK	773
			Australia	679
			Netherlands	502
			France	482
			Ireland	420
216–389	19%	23%	Israel	389
			Czechoslovakia	371
			Finland	348
			Argentina	346
			Uruguay	331
			Venezuela	322
			West Germany	320
			USSR	308
			Poland	300
			Cuba	**296**
			Hungary	269
			South Africa	264
			Portugal	250
			Italy	235
			Austria	216
100–188	12%	6%	Chile	188
			Panama	183
			Colombia	132
			Greece	128
			Mexico	121
			Brazil	112
			Japan	100
			Peru	100

Per Capita GDP Range (USD)	% of World Population	% World Wealth Held	Representative Countries	GDP Per Capita (USD)
40–92	24%	6%	El Salvador	92
			Nicaragua	89
			Iraq	85
			Iran	85
			Paraguay	84
			Honduras	83
			Guatemala	77
			Dominican Republic	75
			India	57
			Bolivia	55
			Haiti	40
25–40	30%	3%	Saudi Arabia	40
			Ecuador	40
			Ethiopia	38
			Thailand	36
			South Korea	35
			China	27
			Indonesia	25

Source: Statistical Office of the United Nations. *National and Per Capita Income in 70 Countries.* New York: Statistical Office of the United Nations, 1950.

Cuba's per capita world income ranking, while very impressive on its own, is particularly powerful when one considers the fact that, as seminal studies by Kravis, Heston, and Summers have pointed out, exchange-rate-based income comparisons across countries typically make the gap between high-income countries and those in the middle income categories seem larger than they are in real purchasing power terms.[2] Table 3 shows the output of a work by Kravis, Heston, and Summers incorporating a comprehensive sample of data for thirty-four countries into a model that converts the nominal exchange-rate-based US dollar GDP per capita figures for these countries, into real GDP per capita figures expressed in "international dollars," as adjusted by the now well-known and universally used concept of purchasing power parity.

Table 3. Income per Capita in 1955 Based on Purchasing Power Parity.

Country	Per Capita GDP Index (in international dollars)	Country	Per Capita GDP Index (in international dollars)
United States	100.0	Colombia	18.7
Uruguay	60.5	Jamaica	18.2
United Kingdom	59.6	Brazil	15.5
Denmark	58.4	Malaysia	15.5
Belgium	55.9	Zambia	15.0
Netherlands	53.8	Iran	13.5
West Germany	53.5	Philippines	11.4
France	50.1	Sri Lanka	10.8
Austria	43.4	South Korea	7.9
Ireland	32.9	Thailand	7.6
Italy	31.4	Kenya	7.4
Spain	31.4	Pakistan	7.3
Mexico	25.6	India	7.0
Japan	21.2	Malawi	4.0

Source: Kravis, Irving, Alan Heston and Robert Summers. *World Product and Income: International Comparisons of Real Gross Product.* Baltimore: Johns Hopkins University Press, 1982. Pg. 15.

These converted figures incorporate adjustments for the relative purchasing power of the currencies of the nations under study, and thus provide more accurate comparisons across countries. While unfortunately this study did not include Cuba, its findings do support the notion that, on a purchasing power–adjusted basis, Cuba's national income per capita was likely to have been even higher in world rankings than the comparison of nominal figures indicates. This is because, as table 3 summarizes, Kravis, Heston and Summers show that, if stated on purchasing power parity basis, the GDP per capita of Uruguay in 1955 was actually the second highest of all the countries studied—behind the Unites States and slightly above the United Kingdom and Denmark.

Given that the income per capita figures in table 2 and a number of other tables throughout this book show Cuba's socioeconomic standing as comparable or superior to Uruguay's in the 1950s, it is not difficult to deduce that, if Cuba had been included in the Kravis, Heston, and

Summers study, the country would have likely ranked similarly high in terms of its purchasing power parity income and, therefore, ahead of an even greater number of the developed nations than those already highlighted in table 1.

Even more directly, studies by Harry Oshima, professor of economics at the University of Hawaii and a research associate at Stanford University, and Jorge Freyre, professor of economics at the University of Puerto Rico, each found that Cuba's official figures significantly underestimated its national income.[3] Oshima's study, which was undertaken in between 1956 and 1957 and is based on 1953 data, arrived at a number of important conclusions. It found that Cuba's per capita income, corrected for the aforementioned understatement, was approximately $430 per annum, which was about the same in nominal terms as Puerto Rico's, which had been a US territory since the Spanish-American War. Adjusting for price levels, Oshima found that Cuba's income was about 10 percent to 20 percent higher than Puerto Rico's in real terms. The study further pointed out that Cuba's income per capita level was equivalent in 1953 to Italy's and that, by 1957, Cuba's real income had grown an incremental 25 percent relative to its 1953 levels.

Notes

1. Venezuela and Uruguay would have been also among the top of the Latin American rankings of the time; however, their figures are not included in table 1 as the exchange rate data available for them for the 1957 period was not a free-floating rate, as was the case for the other countries that were included in the table. It is also worth noting that, while some studies show Venezuela's income per capita as being higher than Cuba's at the time, Venzuelan income was much more concentrated in oil and less distributed among the country's population and thus why the country generally ranked below Cuba across multiple socioeconomic indicators included in this book.

2. Kravis, Irving, Alan Heston, and Robert Summers. *World Product and Income: International Comparisons of Real Gross Product.* Baltimore: Johns Hopkins University Press, 1982. Pg. 9.

3. Oshima, Harry T. "A New Estimate of the National Income and Product of Cuba in 1953." *Food Research Institute Studies.* Palo Alto: Stanford University Food Research Institute, Nov. 1961.In addition, see: Freyre, Jorge F. "The Cuban Economy in the Decade of 1948–1958." *The Cuban Economy: Past, Present and Future.* Ed. Coral Gables: Collegium of Cuban Economists, 1997.

3

Monetary System and Trade in the 1950s

In addition to a country's national income, the strength of its monetary system and the vibrancy of its trade activities are excellent indicators of its overall macroeconomic health and level of development. Wealthier countries have greater levels of financial assets per capita than less wealthy countries. They also tend to have higher levels of foreign reserves per capita. Similarly, economies that are strong and structurally sound will tend to have a more stable currency than less robust economies. In the case of trade, it is also well established that open economies are generally more advanced than those that are less active participants in world commerce. The stronger economies will have a greater national income with which to import and a greater number of competitively advantaged industries from which to export. This chapter will demonstrate that, with regard to both the strength of its monetary system and the vibrancy of its trade activities, Cuba's metrics placed it among the most developed nations in the world.

Monetary System

Three notable facts stand out with regard to the strength of Cuba's monetary system in the 1950s: (i) the value of currency in circulation per capita in Cuba was comparable to that of the world's richest nations; (ii) the value of per capita gold and foreign exchange holdings in the island were among highest in the world; and (iii) the Cuban peso was among the most stable and well-managed currencies in the world.

As highlighted by *Pick's Currency Yearbook*, a country's level of currency per capita is an important measure of its wealth. Based on this measure, *Pick's Currency Yearbook* in 1956[1] separated the countries of the world into high-income countries, middle-income countries, and poor countries. Based on Pick's rankings, Cuba stood solidly among the group of developed nations at the thirteenth spot in the world,

Table 4. Currency in Circulation per Capita in 1956.

Country	Currency in Circulation Per capita (USD)	Country	Currency in Circulation Per capita (USD)
Switzerland	287.6	Japan	20.6
Belgium	244.0	Egypt	20.5
United States	187.0	Saudi Arabia	19.4
France	177.0	Guatemala	19.1
Sweden	147.2	Brazil	18.6
Norway	126.7	Nicaragua	15.5
Canada	126.0	Chile	14.9
Netherlands	118.0	Mexico	14.7
New Zealand	95.4	Thailand	13.0
Australia	95.3	Libya	12.8
United Kingdom	93.2	Peru	12.2
Austria	78.1	Czechoslovakia	11.8
Cuba	**74.1**	Honduras	11.6
Lebanon	72.2	Colombia	11.3
West Germany	71.6	East Germany	11.3
Denmark	71.6	Ecuador	10.5
Ireland	70.6	Philippines	10.3
Iceland	69.1	Turkey	9.3
Argentina	61.5	Ceylon	8.1
Venezuela	61.3	Laos	8.0
Italy	59.0	Viet Nam	7.2
Israel	51.1	India	7.2
Uruguay	49.1	Pakistan	6.5
Portugal	46.9	Bolivia	5.9
Hong Kong	45.5	Iran	5.7
Finland	40.6	Paraguay	5.6
Spain	37.5	Hungary	5.1
Malaya	37.0	Bulgaria	4.9
Surinam	34.4	Haiti	4.8
Jordan	27.6	Taiwan	4.8
Syria	26.7	Poland	4.8

Country	Currency in Circulation Per capita (USD)	Country	Currency in Circulation Per capita (USD)
Costa Rica	26.1	Rumania	4.6
Iraq	25.7	Indonesia	3.8
Greece	24.5	North Korea	3.7
South Africa	24.4	Afghanistan	3.6
USSR	24.2	Burma	3.6
Ghana	21.5	Ethiopia	3.3
El Salvador	21.4	Cambodia	3.1
Dominican Republic	21.3		

Source: Pick Publishing Corporation. *Pick's Currency Yearbook*. New York: Pick Publishing Corporation, 1957. Pg. 23.

ahead of its closest Latin American neighbor, Argentina, by more than 20 percent, and ahead of West Germany, Denmark, Ireland, Italy, Portugal, Spain, Greece, and Japan.

Additionally, Cuba's currency was among the most stable in the world, as it was buttressed by one of the highest levels of gold and foreign exchange reserves per capita in the planet. Cuba's gold reserves per capita were also the thirteenth highest among all of the reporting countries in the world, with nearly double the reserves per capita of the United Kingdom, nearly triple those of France and Italy, and ahead of Greece and Japan by even greater margins.

The strength and stability of the Cuban peso was notable from its establishment in 1914 to the Revolution of 1959. The currency's already-notable stability had been further bolstered by the establishment of the Banco Nacional de Cuba in 1948. During the entirety of the Cuban republican period, the peso never faced currency controls and, nonetheless, always maintained its value right around par with the US dollar, having been slightly weaker than the greenback in the late 1930s and stronger by up to 17 percent in the middle 1940s.

In its in-depth analysis of various world currencies, *Pick's Currency Yearbook* for 1957 compliments the strength, transferability, and stability of the Cuban peso and notes that, thanks to these attributes, the Cuban peso had outperformed even the US dollar over some periods. An important contributor to the steadiness of Cuba's currency was

Table 5. Gold and Foreign Exchange Holdings in 1956.

Country	Total Value of Gold and Foreign Exchange Holdings (millions of USD)	Per Capita Gold & Foreign Exchange Holdings (USD)	Country	Total Value of Gold and Foreign Exchange Holdings (millions of USD)	Per Capita Gold & Foreign Exchange Holdings (USD)
Switzerland	1,894	375.9	Egypt	566	23.9
Venezuela	942	158.2	Guatemala	70	20.9
United States	22,058	130.6	El Salvador	39	17.0
Belgium	1,143	128.1	Japan	1,507	16.8
Canada	1,944	120.9	Mexico	510	16.5
Australia	952	101.0	Syria	62	15.6
Netherlands	1,072	98.4	Thailand	311	15.0
New Zealand	195	89.5	Dominican Rep	37	14.3
Iceland	14	89.4	Iran	229	12.2
West Germany	4,291	84.5	Costa Rica	12	11.9
Ireland	234	80.7	Chile	76	11.0
Portugal	692	78.3	Brazil	612	10.2
Cuba	**479**	**78.1**	Colombia	131	10.1
Uruguay	202	75.5	Turkey	230	9.3
Sweden	473	64.7	Ecuador	32	8.3
Lebanon	88	58.5	Peru	67	6.9
Austria	406	58.1	Philippines	161	6.6

Country			Country		
Iraq	353	55.7	Burma	121	6.1
Malaya	324	53.2	Nicaragua	7	5.4
Norway	179	51.6	Viet-Nam	132	5.0
United Kingdom	2,237	43.5	Paraguay	7	4.6
Finland	174	40.5	South Korea	99	4.4
Denmark	131	29.4	Pakistan	373	4.3
Israel	55	28.2	Indonesia	254	3.0
Italy	1,308	27.1	Yugoslavia	43	2.4
France	1,180	27.0	Spain	57	2.0
Greece	211	26.3	Bolivia	5	1.6
South Africa	372	26.0	India	360	0.9
Ceylon	221	24.8			

Source: Gold and Foreign Exchange Reserves are from: Statistical Office of the United Nations, Department of Economic and Social Affairs. *Statistical Yearbook 1958.* New York: Statistical Office of the United Nations, 1958. Pg. 451. This applies in all cases except for France and the United Kingdom, which are from: Statistical Office of the United Nations, Department of Economic and Social Affairs. *Statistical Yearbook 1961.* New York: Statistical Office of the United Nations, 1961. Pg. 521. The population data used for all countries in the world to arrive at per capita values is from the Statistical Office of the United Nations, Department of Economic and Social Affairs. *Demographic Yearbook 1961.* New York: Statistical Office of the United Nations, 1961. 126, except for that of Cuba. The population figure utilized for Cuba is that reported for the year under analysis by the Cuban National. Bank in: Banco Nacional de Cuba. *Memoria 1958–59.* Havana: Banco Nacional de Cuba, 1959. 95.

Table 6. Inflation Rates in 1957.

Country	% chg. in CPI	Country	% chg. in CPI
Iraq	-4.4%	Poland	3.2%
Burma	-3.6%	Yugoslavia	3.4%
South Korea	-3.1%	South Africa	3.6%
Viet-Nam	-2.3%	Angola	3.0%
Singapore	-2.1%	**Cuba**	**3.1%**
Germany East	-2.1%	Germany West	3.8%
Dominican Rep	-1.9%	Pakistan	3.8%
Japan	-0.9%	Nicaragua	4.1%
Iran	-0.7%	New Zealand	4.4%
Bulgaria	0.0%	Ireland	4.5%
Czechoslovakia	0.0%	Cyprus	4.7%
Haiti	0.0%	India	4.8%
Hungary	0.0%	Jamaica	4.9%
Nigeria	0.0%	Thailand	5.1%
Panama	0.0%	Venezuela	5.1%
Taiwan	0.8%	Sweden	5.3%
Australia	0.9%	Norway	5.4%
Belgium	0.9%	Iceland	5.8%
Luxemburg	0.9%	El Salvador	5.9%
Portugal	1.0%	Paraguay	6.2%
Ecuador	1.0%	Cambodia	6.3%
Greece	1.6%	Finland	6.7%
Kenya	1.7%	Laos	7.5%
Mozambique	1.7%	Peru	8.0%
Austria	1.8%	Sudan	8.4%
Canada	1.9%	Lebanon	9.6%
Switzerland	1.9%	Cameroons	10.7%
Guatemala	1.9%	Ceylon	11.1%
USSR	2.1%	Mexico	11.1%
United Kingdom	2.6%	Algeria	12.3%
Greenland	2.7%	Turkey	12.5%
Costa Rica	2.7%	Spain	13.8%
Italy	2.7%	France	14.2%
Honduras	2.8%	Colombia	15.0%

Country	% chg. in CPI	Country	% chg. in CPI
Puerto Rico	2.8%	Brazil	15.0%
United States	2.9%	Uruguay	17.4%
Bolivia	2.9%	Chile	19.9%
Philippines	2.9%	Argentina	31.5%
Israel	3.0%	Indonesia	45.8%

Source: Calculated based on the change in cost of living index between 1956 and 1957 as reported by: Statistical Office of the United Nations, Department of Economic and Social Affairs. *Statistical Yearbook 1959*. New York: Statistical Office of the United Nations, 1959. Pg. 440. Statistical Office of the United Nations, Department of Economic and Social Affairs. *Statistical Yearbook 1960*. New York: Statistical Office of the United Nations, 1960. Pg. 451.

Table 7. Cuba's Annual Federal Fiscal Budget (1940 to 1958).

Year	Receipts	Expenses	Surplus/ (Deficit)
1940	78,146	79,347	(1,201)
1941	80,165	77,678	2,487
1942	106,307	101,705	4,602
1943	125,315	112,229	13,086
1944	148,423	133,188	15,235
1945	158,018	145,146	12,872
1946	201,065	174,014	27,051
1947	277,248	199,386	77,862
1948	241,862	288,794	(46,932)
1949/50[1]	229,587	228,615	972
1950/51	285,913	271,427	14,486
1951/52	327,534	325,211	2,323
1952/53	309,459	340,585	(31,126)
1953/54	270,212	303,513	(33,301)
1954/55	303,381	329,255	(25,874)
1955/56	328,734	325,317	3,417
1956/57	370,843	354,694	16,149
1957/58	387,044	385,554	1,490
Cumulative	4,229,256	4,175,658	53,598

Source: Cuban Economic Research Project, University of Miami. A Study on Cuba. Coral Gables: University of Miami Press, 1965. pg. 871.
[1] Fiscal year starting July 1st , 1949, to June 30,1950.

the price stability that Cuba was able to maintain during its republican period, with the island's consumer price index (CPI) consistently being held in check between 0 and 3 percent. As table 6 shows, between 1956 and 1957, for example, one of the years with higher inflation in Cuba during the decade of the 1950s, Cuba's inflation rate was only 3.1 percent, comparable to the level of inflation seen in the United States, and in stark contrast to inflation in the teens for Spain, France, Brazil, and Chile, and over 30 percent for Argentina. Simultaneously, Cuba was also able to avoid the troublesome deflation that afflicted several countries during the period.[2]

Another important contributor to monetary and overall financial stability, the country's fiscal condition, had been maintained in healthy balance with frequent fiscal budget surpluses and infrequent deficits. In fact, between 1940 and 1958, there were only five years when Cuba had a budget deficit, and on a cumulative basis, the country accumulated a $54 million budget surplus, a significant figure both for the times and relative to the size of the country's annual budget (table 7).

As the decade of the 1950s came to a close, only seven of the major eighty-five currencies in circulation in the world had existed without a legal devaluation for more than twenty years—the Cuban peso was one of those seven.[3]

Trade

Table 8 confirms that, as mentioned previously, the poorest countries in the world in the 1950s—such as Haiti, India, and Nigeria—also place toward the bottom of world rankings in terms of trade per capita. In contrast, developed countries such as Switzerland, Canada, Sweden, the United Kingdom, West Germany, and the United States all rank toward the top of the world's standings. This is consistent with the fact that for countries to be active trade participants they need to have the requisite national income to afford high levels of imports and must enjoy sufficient comparative advantages relative to other nations of the world in order to make its exports attractive in world markets. Cuba's economy had advanced to the point where both of these elements were very much features of its economy. In fact, Cuba ranked ahead of France, Portugal, Italy, Spain, and even the United States, in terms of the value of foreign commerce that it transacted on a per capita basis.

Also, beyond the total value of trade that took place, Cuba's trade balance was reflective of the fact that the island's foreign commerce was very much a two-sided affair, and not driven by trade deficits. While Cuba

Table 8. Trade Volumes per Capita in 1957.

Country	Imports (mm of USD)	Exports (mm of USD)	Value of Total Trade (mm USD)	Total Trade per capita (USD)	Country	Imports (mm of USD)	Exports (mm of USD)	Value of Total Trade (mm USD)	Total Trade per capita (USD)
Iceland	84	61	145	879	Jordan	126	16	142	93
Greenland	13	9	22	759	Greece	525	220	745	92
New Zealand	832	772	1604	720	Bulgaria	332	370	702	92
Switzerland	1,964	1,560	3,524	689	Libya	79	15	94	82
Venezuela	1,668	2,366	4,034	658	Ceylon	379	359	738	81
Netherlands	4,105	3,097	7,202	653	Japan	4,284	2,877	7,161	79
Canada	5,710	5,094	10,804	651	Poland	1,251	975	2,226	79
Sweden	2,428	2,137	4,565	620	Guatemala	147	114	261	76
Norway	1,275	821	2096	600	Colombia	483	511	994	75
Denmark	1,358	1,147	2505	558	Peru	400	320	720	73
Hong Kong	901	529	1,430	554	Mexico	1,155	727	1,882	59
Australia	1,684	2,203	3,887	403	Yugoslavia	661	395	1,056	59
Finland	891	826	1,717	396	Ecuador	89	133	222	56
United Kingdom	10,960	9,266	20,226	392	Albania	53	29	82	56
West Germany	7,499	8,575	16,074	312	Angola	123	117	240	54
Ireland	516	368	884	306	Bolivia	92	74	166	50
Austria	1,128	979	2107	301	Brazil	1,488	1,392	2,880	47
Israel	436	142	578	298	Spain	862	476	1,338	45
Cuba	**813**	**845**	**1,658**	**271**	Romania	415	390	805	45

(Continued)

Table 8. (Continued)

Country	Imports (mm of USD)	Exports (mm of USD)	Value of Total Trade (mm USD)	Total Trade per capita (USD)	Country	Imports (mm of USD)	Exports (mm of USD)	Value of Total Trade (mm USD)	Total Trade per capita (USD)
France	6,110	5,065	11175	253	Egypt	547	493	1,040	43
Portugal	1,964	288	2252	253	Philippines	613	431	1,044	41
United States	13,109	20,682	33791	197	Turkey	661	345	1,006	39
South Africa	1,539	1,264	2803	191	China (Taiwan)	212	148	360	38
Costa Rica	103	83	186	180	Thailand	407	365	772	37
Uruguay	255	128	383	141	Paraguay	27	33	60	36
Panama	99	36	135	139	Pakistan	2,243	358	2,601	30
Italy	3,674	2,550	6224	128	Mozambique	104	65	169	27
Chile	441	458	899	126	Burma	296	229	525	26
Hungary	683	488	1171	119	Laos	42	1	43	26
Argentina	1,310	975	2285	115	Cambodia	58	52	110	24
Nicaragua	81	64	145	109	Nigeria	427	357	784	24
El Salvador	115	139	254	108	Haiti	40	34	74	22
Iraq	341	360	701	107	Indonesia	803	970	1,773	21
Ghana	271	229	500	105	India	2,243	1,379	3,622	9
Dominican Rep	117	161	278	103					

Source: Trade data are from: Statistical Office of the United Nations, Department of Economic and Social Affairs. *Statistical Yearbook 1960*. New York: Statistical Office of the United Nations, 1960. Pg. 386. The population figures utilized in order to arrive at per capita values are from the Statistical Office of the United Nations, Department of Economic and Social Affairs. *Demographic Yearbook 1961*. New York: Statistical Office of the United Nations, 1961. Pg. 126–137. The prior source is for all countries, except Cuba. The population figure utilized for Cuba is that reported for the year under analysis in Banco Nacional de Cuba. *Memoria 1958–59*. Havana: Banco Nacional de Cuba, 1959. Pg. 95.

Table 9. Imports per Capita in 1957.

Country	Imports per capita (USD)	Country	Imports per capita (USD)
Iceland	509.1	Nicaragua	60.8
Greenland	448.3	Ghana	56.9
Switzerland	383.8	Iraq	52.2
New Zealand	373.3	El Salvador	48.9
Netherlands	372.5	Japan	47.2
Norway	364.9	Poland	44.2
Hong Kong	348.8	Bulgaria	43.4
Canada	344.2	Dominican Rep	43.3
Sweden	329.6	Guatemala	42.6
Denmark	302.6	Ceylon	41.4
Venezuela	271.9	Peru	40.3
Israel	225.1	Yugoslavia	36.7
Portugal	220.5	Colombia	36.5
United Kingdom	212.2	Albania	36.3
Finland	205.5	Mexico	36.2
Ireland	178.9	Spain	29.3
Australia	174.7	Bolivia	27.7
Austria	161.2	Angola	27.4
Surinam	147.7	Turkey	25.9
West Germany	145.7	Pakistan	25.7
France	138.6	Laos	25.4
Cuba	**132.6**	Brazil	24.3
South Africa	104.9	Philippines	24.2
Czechoslovakia	103.8	Romania	23.3
Panama	101.7	Ecuador	22.7
Costa Rica	99.7	Egypt	22.6
East Germany	98.5	China (Taiwan)	22.3
Uruguay	93.6	Thailand	19.3
Jordan	82.5	Mozambique	16.9
United States	76.3	Paraguay	16.4

(Continued)

Table 9. (Continued)

Country	Imports per capita (USD)	Country	Imports per capita (USD)
Italy	75.8	Burma	14.8
Hungary	69.3	Nigeria	12.9
Libya	68.5	Cambodia	12.6
Argentina	65.9	Haiti	11.8
Greece	64.8	Indonesia	9.4
Chile	61.9	India	5.5

Source: The level of imports per capita was calculated from data gathered from the Statistical Office of the United Nations, Department of Economic and Social Affairs. *Statistical Yearbook 1960.* New York: Statistical Office of the United Nations, 1960. Table 1. The population figures utilized in order to arrive at per capita values are from: Statistical Office of the United Nations, Department of Economic and Social Affairs. *Demographic Yearbook 1961.* New York: Statistical Office of the United Nations, 1961. Pg. 126–137. Previous source is for all countries except Cuba. The population figure utilized for Cuba is that reported in: Banco Nacional de Cuba. *Memoria 1958–59.* Havana: Banco Nacional de Cuba, 1959. Pg. 95.

Table 10. Balance of Trade per Capita in 1957.

Country	Balance of Trade (in millions of dollars)	Surplus or Deficit in trade per capita (in US dollars)
Venezuela	698	113.8
Australia	519	53.8
United States	7,573	44.1
West Germany	1,076	20.9
Dominican Rep	44	16.3
East Germany	196	12.0
El Salvador	24	10.2
Cuba	**32**	**5.2**
Spain	-386	-13.1
Mexico	-428	-13.4
Finland	-65	-15.0
Japan	-1,407	-15.5
Argentina	-335	-16.9
South Africa	-275	-18.7
Costa Rica	-20	-19.4

Country	Balance of Trade (in millions of dollars)	Surplus or Deficit in trade per capita (in US dollars)
Austria	-149	-21.3
Pakistan	-1,885	-21.6
Italy	-1,124	-23.2
France	-1,045	-23.7
New Zealand	-60	-26.9
United Kingdom	-1,694	-32.8
Canada	-616	-37.1
Greece	-305	-37.7
Sweden	-291	-39.5
Uruguay	-127	-46.6
Denmark	-211	-47.0
Ireland	-148	-51.3
Libya	-64	-55.5
Panama	-63	-64.7
Jordan	-110	-72.0
Switzerland	-404	-79.0
Netherlands	-1,008	-91.5
Norway	-454	-129.9
Greenland	-4	-137.9
Iceland	-23	-139.4
Hong Kong	-372	-144.0
Israel	-294	-151.8
Portugal	-1,676	-188.1

enjoyed some of the highest levels of imports per capita in the world (table 9), it also exported more than most countries on a per capita basis. As a result, since the 1930s trade surpluses were not only part of Cuba's normal pattern of economic activity, but they were among the highest in the world on a per capita basis.[4] Table 10, for example, illustrates that, in 1957, a year when the Cuba's trade surplus was toward the lower end of its typical range, Cuba's per capita trade surplus was only surpassed by seven countries.

Notes

1. Pick Publishing Corporation. *Pick's Currency Yearbook 1957.* New York: Pick Publishing Corporation, 1957. Pg. 23.
2. From an economic growth standpoint, the advantage of moderate inflation has been well established. For further evidence the record on inflation in Cuba during de 1950s, generally between 1 and 2 percent a year, see
3. *Pick's Currency Yearbook,* op. cit., pg. 24.
4. Banco Nacional de Cuba, op. cit.

4

Economic Participation and Standards of Living in the 1950s

Cuba's developmental achievements throughout its republican period were most important because of the positive impact that this development had broadly on the island's population. Cuba's development allowed for two important things to happen. Firstly, as the economy advanced and became more sophisticated, a larger proportion of the country's population participated in the country's economic output through increasing portions of GDP being paid in wages to a broad cross-section of the population. This greater wage participation coincided with increasing wage levels that provided the population with purchasing power levels that allowed it to access a greater quantity and higher quality of goods and services and thus ever-growing levels of utility. Indeed, as this chapter will demonstrate, by the end of the 1950s Cuba had attained levels of economic participation, wages, and consumption of high-quality goods and services that were comparable to those enjoyed, at the time, by the populations of some of the most advanced nations in the world.

Wages and Income Distribution

Even in the most advanced societies, income differentials are entirely natural. The difference between the income that one person earns in a free-market society vs. that which is earned by another is determined by the value that society *freely* places on each individual's productive activities. These different attributions of value will lead to individuals being able to fetch different income levels within the same occupation and across different occupations. The engineer whose inventive genius leads to the development of a solution to a problem faced by many will likely earn a higher income than the engineer whose job is to design and perfect only a small component of that same solution. The star professional baseball player whose rare talent and years of arduous practice leads him to be in a position where he is able to fill stadiums and entertain millions on television will earn a higher income than the more easily replaceable person whose job is to sell tickets at the box office. And, the entrepreneur, who at great risk builds a successful enterprise that solves an otherwise unmet need in society, will earn a higher income than the business-school graduate who takes a job at the entrepreneur's firm and benefits from the steady paycheck that the entrepreneur's enterprise provides.

All of the aforementioned differences in earnings are normal and healthy features of free markets because they reflect the net result of many individual choices. There are times, however, when differences in income arise from structural limitations that curtail the economic development of a country in comparison to its full potential. Two of the most important structural limitations that can lead to unhealthy income differentials are: (i) uneven access to education and (ii) uneven access to capital. Uneven access to education can keep individuals from being able to fully blossom their innate talents, thus limiting their ability to innovate and contribute to the productivity and utility of a society. This, in turn, limits the income potential not only of those individuals but of society as a whole. Similarly, a mismatch between good ideas and capital can keep potential entrepreneurs and innovators from bringing about advancements that would improve society as a whole and simultaneously bring to that individual entrepreneur the higher levels of income that his talents would merit.

While Cuba, and the entire world for that matter, had a lot of room for improvement in the 1950s with respect to access to educational opportunities and financing, both of these elements had become available broadly enough in Cuba by the 1950s—again, relative to other countries of the world and in the context of the time period—to provide for the fruitful participation of many in the country's economy. This broad participation resulted in Cuba's national income being widely distributed among a large cross section of Cuban society. *Investment in Cuba*, a thorough study of the Cuban economy that the United States Department of Commerce published in 1956, concluded that "subsistence living, so prevalent in many areas of Latin America (not to mention the world), is not characteristic of Cuba, whose national income reflects the wage economy of the country."[1] Consistent with

Table 11. Percentage of GDP Paid as Compensation to Employees in 1956.

Country	% of GDP Paid as Compensation to Workers	Country	% of GDP Paid as Compensation to Workers
United Kingdom	73.0%	Netherlands	55.3%
United States	69.8%	Belgium	54.5%
Canada	65.0%	Italy	51.8%
Sweden	64.4%	Congo	49.9%
Cuba	**64.0%**	Honduras	49.4%
Finland	62.3%	China (Taiwan)	49.3%
Switzerland	61.9%	Ecuador	49.3%
Australia	60.4%	Japan	48.9%
Germany West	60.4%	Brazil	47.9%
Austria	60.0%	Ceylon	47.4%
Costa Rica	59.0%	Chile[1]	46.0%
France	59.0%	Philippines	41.8%
Luxemburg	58.5%	Kenya	40.3%
Norway	57.8%	Peru	40.0%
Denmark	57.6%	Colombia	39.2%
Argentina	57.3%	Greece	38.0%
Ireland	57.2%	Cyprus	32.9%
New Zealand	57.2%	Uganda	20.3%
South Africa	56.7%		

Source: International Labor Office (ILO). *Yearbook of Labour Statistics 1962.* Geneva: International Labor Office, 1962. Pg. 407.
[1]from: Statistical Office of the United Nations, Department of Economic and Social Affairs. *Monthly Bulletin of Statistics.* New York: Statistical Office of the United Nations, November, 1957.

this affirmation, table 11 shows that Cuba's share of GDP paid as wages placed the island among the top of the world rankings and, therefore, in the company of some of the most advanced and equitable economies in the world.

Additionally, Cuba's economic activities were sufficiently deep and varied to support a high labor force participation rate. Indeed, by the end of the 1950s, Cuba's labor force participation (53.8 percent) was almost exactly the same as in the United States. Furthermore,

Table 12. Sample Wages in the Industrial Sector in Cuba in 1955.

	Minimum Hourly Wage Declared by a Respondent (pesos)[1]	Maximum Hourly Wage Declared by a Respondent (pesos)[1]	Average Hourly Wage (pesos)[1]	Average Daily Equivalent (pesos)[1]
Laborer (unskilled gardening, janitoring, heavy unskilled work)	0.71	1.07	0.92	7.36
Loader helper (filling and emptying containers; loading and unloading trucks, tank cars, box cars)	0.87	1.36	1.08	8.64
Mechanic's helper (lubricating trucks and autos; melting tin bars; operating winch when small loads are involved; doing chores for mechanics)	0.72	1.23	1.05	8.40
Mechanic third class (putting packing in machinery; sharpening blades in machinery; fitting and removing dies; soldering; repairs of auto and truck springs; changing tires; repairing factory trolleys; repairing air tubes)	0.99	1.46	1.2	9.60
Mechanic second class (repairing pumps, valves, and tools, dismantling engines, boilers, and trucks and automobiles; changing wheels; adjusting bearings; installing, repairing, maintaining, testing, and calibrating valves, dials, and other measuring devices)	1.08	1.61	1.3	10.40

	Minimum Hourly Wage Declared by a Respondent (pesos)[1]	Maximum Hourly Wage Declared by a Respondent (pesos)[1]	Average Hourly Wage (pesos)[1]	Average Daily Equivalent (pesos)[1]
Mechanic first class (machinist; auto mechanic; mechanic repairing air equipment, sensitive or complex machinery, etc.	1.25	1.83	1.45	11.60

Source: United States Department of Commerce. *Investments in Cuba: Basic Information for United States Businessmen.* Washington DC: US Government Printing Office, 1956. Pg. 86.

Notes: [1] The Cuban peso was at par with the US dollar

23 percent of Cuba's workforce consisted of skilled labor, a rate that was comparable to that achieved by developed nations. Also at par with developed nations was the high degree of unionization that labor had achieved in the country.[2] All of these elements, combined with the establishment and enforcement of a very comprehensive minimum wage standard,[3] provided Cuba with a strong and developed labor market, and with average wages that were among the highest in the world. The minimum wage schedule was updated periodically to take into account regional increases in the cost of living. As of 1958, Public Order Number 190, of April 14 of that year, set the schedule of minimum daily wages as follows: $3.30 in Havana and Marianao; $3.10 in other cities; and $2.90 in rural areas.[4] Since, as was noted earlier, the cost of living in Cuba was exceptionally stable through the decade of the 1950s, this schedule was not significantly different from previous ones.

As can be seen in table 12, a survey conducted by the American embassy in Havana, and which the US Department of Commerce presented to potential investors in *Investment in Cuba* as a guide for the typical level of wages that they should expect to pay if engaging in business in Cuba, showed that, in 1955, typical salaries received in the industrial sector of the economy, were significantly above the minimum wages in place in 1958.

The sample wages in table 12, above, agree with the findings of a study by the U.N. International Labor Organization (ILO) in 1959,

Table 13. Industrial Wages in 1958.

Country	Daily Wage (USD)
United States	16.80
Canada	11.73
Sweden	8.10
Switzerland	8.00
New Zealand	6.72
Denmark	6.46
Norway	6.10
Cuba	**6.00**
Australia	5.82
England	5.75

Source: International Labor Review. International Labor Organization (ILO) *Statistical Supplement July 1959*. Geneva: International Labor Office, 1959.

Table 14. Agricultural Wages in 1958.

Country	Daily Wage (USD)
Canada	7.18
United States	6.80
New Zealand	6.72
Australia	6.61
Sweden	5.47
Norway	4.38
Cuba	**3.00**
West Germany	2.57
Ireland	2.25
Denmark	2.03

Source: International Labor Review. International Labor Organization (ILO) *Statistical Supplement July 1959*. Geneva: International Labor Office, 1959.

which determined that in that year the average industrial wage in the island was $6.00 per day. As can be seen in table 13, this places Cuba in the company of the most developed countries in the world. The same study placed the average daily agricultural wage of the country at $3.00, which, while not as far ahead of the Cuban minimum wage for rural areas, was, as can be observed in table 14, also among the highest in the world.

Table 15. Unemployment Rates in 1958.

Country	% Unemployed
Switzerland	0.5%
Japan	1.3%
United Kingdom	2.2%
Netherlands	2.4%
Sweden	2.5%
Germany West	3.5%
Cuba	**4.7%**
Austria	5.3%
United States	6.8%
Canada	7.1%
Belgium	8.5%
Ireland	8.6%
Italy	9.0%
Denmark	9.6%
Puerto Rico	13.9%

Source: Value for Cuba is from: Cuban Economic Research Project, University of Miami. *A Study on Cuba*. Coral Gables: University of Miami Press, 1965. Pg. 1544. The rest of the countries' data are from: International Labor Organization (ILO). *Statistical Supplement July 1959*. Geneva: International Labor Office, 1959. Pg. 2 and: Statistical Office of the United Nations, Department of Economic and Social Affairs. *Monthly Bulletin of Statistics*. New York: Statistical Office of the United Nations, 1960. Pg. 17.

Finally, while the data is scarce with regard to the percentages of the working-age population that were unemployed in the different countries of the world in the 1950s, the evidence that is available does point to Cuba having an unemployment rate that was below that of the two most developed countries in the Americas, the United States and Canada, and below all of the countries of the Caribbean and Latin America (table 15).

Consumption and Purchasing Power

As the statistics of wages and prices have firmly established, the purchasing power of Cuban industrial and agricultural wages was comparatively among the highest in the world. Further supporting evidence of this conclusion can be seen by consulting table 16, which shows that the purchasing power of these wages over the principal

Table 16. Purchasing Power of Income Received by a Worker for a Half-Day of Labor in the 1950s.

Purchasing Power of Money Earned by a Worker for Half Day of Work					
	Eggs	Sugar	Bread	Butter	Meat
United States	20	4,290	2,500	650	1,000
Cuba	**7**	**2,600**	**1,500**	**380**	**390**
England	6	1,580	1,600	410	330
Mexico	5	1,450	900	130	250
Soviet Union	3	215	1,400	80	200
Czechoslovakia	2	315	1,500	80	160
Poland	2	300	1,100	80	220

Source: Illan, Jose M. Cuba: *Facts and Figures of an Economy in Ruins*. Trans. George A. Wehby. Miami: Editorial ATP, 1964. Pg. 29.

foodstuffs a worker typically consumed was higher in Cuba than all of the other countries included in the study, with the exception of the United States.

Moreover, as table 17 makes clear, Cubans took advantage of that purchasing power to achieve a very healthy daily caloric intake. As that table shows, by the end of the decade of the 1940s (the latest available data point for this particular metric in UN publications published prior to the Revolution), Cubans had the same caloric intake as Germans, a developed economy even immediately post its defeat in WWII, and higher than Israel, Austria, Greece, Italy, Portugal, and Japan, not to mention all of its Latin American peers, other than Argentina and Uruguay, which were large producers of meat.

In addition to these impressive achievements in terms of food consumption, the tables that we present in the rest of this chapter corroborate that the purchasing power of the median Cuban citizen was not only sufficient to allow him plentiful consumption of food, but in fact allowed him to achieve a broad purchasing power that covered many more consumer goods and services.

The first example of this is the high level of automobile usage that Cubans were able to achieve. Purchasing an automobile requires a significant outlay of capital relative to most other consumer items, and thus a high number of passenger automobiles per capita indicates that a significant proportion of the population had been able to achieve a high level of disposable income. It is thus particularly impressive that Cuba had been able to purchase more automobiles per capita in the 1950s

Table 17. Calories Consumed per Day, 1948–1953.

Country	Calories Consumed Per Day	Year	Country	Calories Consumed Per Day	Year
Ireland	3,430	1948–50	Yugoslavia	2,650	1951–53
New Zealand	3,370	1948–50	South Africa	2,630	1948–50
Denmark	3,230	1948–50	Turkey	2,530	1948–50
Iceland	3,230	1948–50	Cyprus	2,500	1948–49
Australia	3,230	1948–50	Greece	2,490	1948–50
United States	3,180	1948–50	Chile	2,420	1951–52
Switzerland	3,170	1948–50	Mexico	2,380	1954–56
Sweden	3,150	1948–50	Egypt	2,370	1948–50
United Kingdom	3,130	1948–50	Brazil	2,370	1951–52
Canada	3,110	1948–50	Columbia	2,370	1948–49
Norway	3,100	1948–50	Italy	2,350	1948–50
Finland	2,980	1949–50	Portugal	2,320	1948–50
Argentina	2,970	1951–53	Venezuela	2,160	1949–50
Uruguay	2,950	1952–53	Pakistan	2,040	1951–53
Netherlands	2,940	1948–50	Honduras	1,990	1948–50
Belgium	2,890	1948–50	China	1,980	1948–50
France	2,800	1948–50	Ceylon	1,970	1952–53
Cuba	**2,730**	**1948–49**	Philippines	1,940	1952–53
Germany	2,730	1948–50	Japan	1,870	1948–50
Israel	2,680	1950–51	India	1,750	1951–53
Austria	2,670	1948–50			

Source: Statistical Office of the United Nations, Department of Economic and Social Affairs. *Statistical Yearbook 1959.* New York: Statistical Office of the United Nations, 1959. Pg. 298.

than the inhabitants of most other countries in the world, including Italy, Portugal, Spain, and Japan (see table 18).

Similarly, the development of a profitable and vibrant private television industry, especially back in the decade of the 1950s, was reserved for nations that had achieved important and widespread levels of economic prosperity. This was the case for several reasons. First, the

Table 18. Inhabitants per Passenger Vehicle in 1957.

Country	Passenger Vehicles (000 units)	Inhabitants per Passenger Vehicle (units)	Country	Passenger Vehicles (000 units)	Inhabitants per Passenger Vehicle (units)
United States	55,906	3.1	Israel	20	96.4
Canada	3,383	4.9	Libya	10	118.9
New Zealand	443	5.0	Chile	54	132.1
Australia	1,564	6.2	Kenya	50	134.4
Yugoslavia	2,200	8.2	Brazil	446	137.3
Sweden	863	8.5	Peru	64	154.1
France [1]	3,972	11.1	Colombia	81	162.9
Luxembourg	28	11.2	El Salvador	14	164.3
United Kingdom	4,205	12.3	Nicaragua	8	170.8
Iceland	12	13.9	Spain	167	176.7
Switzerland	361	14.2	Guatemala	17	203.0
Belgium	633	14.3	Angola	21	209.5
Denmark	280	16.0	Iraq	26	252.4
Ireland	140	20.5	Greece	31	259.5
West Germany	2,453	21.0	Bolivia	12	279.3
South Africa	692	21.2	Paraguay[1]	6	290.9
Norway	153	22.8	Dominican Republic	9	293.9
Singapore	51	28.2	Ghana	15	328.5
Netherlands	376	29.3	Jordan	4	355.1
Austria	233	30.0	Philippines	71	358.2
Venezuela	186	33.0	Egypt	66	365.8
Finland	127	34.2	Iran	49	389.8
Cuba	**158**	**38.8**	Japan	219	415.2
Italy	1,231	39.4	Honduras	4	421.2
Lebanon	30	50.8	Poland	62	457.2
Uruguay	52	51.1	Lao's PDR	3	551.7

Country	Passenger Vehicles (000 units)	Inhabitants per Passenger Vehicle (units)	Country	Passenger Vehicles (000 units)	Inhabitants per Passenger Vehicle (units)
Argentina	365	54.4	Haiti	6	564.0
Panama	15	65.3	Ecuador	6	623.7
Costa Rica	14	76.0	Thailand	31	675.5
Portugal	116	76.8	Turkey	37	692.9
Malaya, Fed. Of	73	86.1	Nigeria	23	1468.3
Mexico	366	87.2	India[2]	220	1864.8
Algeria	116	87.4	Pakistan	34	2562.5

Source: Vehicle data is from: Statistical Office of the United Nations, Department of Economic and Social Affairs. *Statistical Yearbook 1961*. New York: Statistical Office of the United Nations, 1961. Pg. 338. The population figures utilized in order to arrive at a number of inhabitants per passenger vehicle are from: Statistical Office of the United Nations, Department o f Economic and Social Affairs. *Demographic Yearbook 1961*. New York: Statistical Office of the United Nations, 1961. Pg. 126–137. The aforementioned source is for all countries except Cuba. The population figure utilized for Cuba is that reported for the year under analysis in: Banco Nacional de Cuba. *Memoria 1958–59*. Havana: Banco Nacional de Cuba, 1959. Pg. 95. Notes: 1 1958; 2 1956.

television industry requires a major amount of capital investment in infrastructure, and also a significant amount of investment by consumers, for whom the purchase of a television set was a major outlay that could not be considered until a number of other needs were thoroughly met. Also, since the financing of private television stations depends highly on advertising revenue, the number that a country can support is closely correlated to its level of economic activity and development and, consequently, the overall consumption spending of the population. This is because the larger the consumption that a country can support, the greater the number of companies that will market their products, and thus the more advertising that they will do—providing the revenue necessary to support the operations of television stations. Thus, what can be observed in the two tables that follow is further corroboration of Cuba's overall economic development, and the corresponding level of sophistication it had achieved as a society as the decade of the 1950s came to a close. Firstly, Cuba had more television stations per million inhabitants than any other country

Table 19. Television Stations per Million Inhabitants in 1955.

Country	Number of Television Stations (units)	Television Stations Per Million Inhabitants (units)	Country	Number of Television Stations (units)	Television Stations Per Million Inhabitants (units)
Cuba	**23**	**3.85**	Hong Kong[3]	1	0.36
Luxemburg	1	3.29	Colombia	4	0.32
United States	482	2.90	United Kingdom	16	0.31
Canada	26	1.66	Italy	15	0.31
Syria[3]	6	1.40	Sweden	2	0.28
West Germany	68	1.36	France	11	0.25
Japan	7	0.79	Finland	1	0.24
Switzerland	3	0.60	Netherlands	2	0.19
Austria	4	0.57	Portugal[1]	1	0.11
Australia[1]	5	0.53	Brazil[2]	6	0.10
Venezuela	3	0.52	Philippines	2	0.08
Belgium	4	0.45	Czechoslovakia	1	0.08
Denmark	2	0.45	Argentina	1	0.05
Mexico	12	0.40	Thailand	1	0.05
Dominican Rep	1	0.40	Spain	1	0.03
Uruguay[1]	1	0.37			

Source: The number of television stations is from: Statistical Office of the United Nations, Department of Economic and Social Affairs. *Statistical Yearbook 1960.* New York: Statistical Office of the United Nations, 1960. Pg. 610. The population figures utilized in order to arrive at the per one million inhabitants are from: Statistical Office of the United Nations, Department of Economic and Social Affairs. *Demographic Yearbook 1961.* New York: Statistical Office of the United Nations, 1961. Pg. 126–137. Citation is for all countries except Cuba. The population figure utilized for Cuba is that reported for the year under analysis by: Banco Nacional de Cuba. *Memoria 1958–59.* Havana: Banco Nacional de Cuba, 1959. Pg. 95.
Notes: [1] 1956; [2] 1957; [3] 1958

Table 20. Inhabitants per Television Receivers in 1956.

Country	Number of Television Receivers (000 units)	Inhabitants per TV Receiver (units)	Country	Number of Television Receivers (000 units)	Inhabitants per TV Receiver (units)
United States	42,000	4	Guatemala	8	394
Canada	2,450	7	Panama	2	474
United Kingdom	6,570	8	Sweden	13	563
Cuba	275	22	Ireland[1]	4	730
Belgium	150	60	Austria	6	1,164
Venezuela	100	60	Finland	2	1,716
West Germany	704	72	El Salvador	1	2,268
France	442	99	Philippines	10	2,451
Denmark	44	102	Uruguay	1	2,675
Netherlands	99	110	Thailand	7	2,955
Mexico	250	124	Yugoslavia	4	4,448
Italy	367	132	Poland	5	5,564
Czechoslovakia	60	221	Spain	3	9,734
East Germany	70	237	Iraq	0.6	10,572
Switzerland	20	252	Norway	0.3	11,540
Colombia	50	259	Bulgaria	0.5	15,152
Argentina	75	260	Hungary	0.6	16,473
Japan	328	274	Portugal	0.3	29,457
Brazil	200	299	Romania	0.5	35,166
Luxemburg	1	306	Algeria	0.1	99,620
Australia	27	349	Turkey	0.1	24,7710
Dominican Rep	7	373			

Source: The number of television units is from: Statistical Office of the United Nations, Department of Economic and Social Affairs. *Statistical Yearbook 1957*. New York: Statistical Office of the United Nations. Pg. 643. The population figures utilized in order to arrive at a number of inhabitants per television set are from: Statistical Office of the United Nations, Department of Economic and Social Affairs. *Demographic Yearbook 1961*. New York: Statistical Office of the United Nations, 1961. Pg. 126–137. Aforementioned source is for all countries except Cuba. The population figure utilized for Cuba is that reported in: Banco Nacional de Cuba. *Memoria 1958–59*. Havana: Banco Nacional de Cuba, 1959. Pg. 95.
Notes: [1] 1955

Table 21. Radio Stations per Million Inhabitants in 1956.

Country	Number	Radio Stations per Million Inhabitants (units)	Country	Number	Radio Stations per Million Inhabitants (units)
Panama	59	62.2	Israel	8	4.1
Costa Rica	38	38.5	Portugal[1]	33	3.8
Uruguay	79	29.5	Angola	16	3.6
Cuba	**160**	**26.4**	Argentina[1]	64	3.3
United States	3,504	20.8	Greece	18	2.2
Dominican Rep[1]	43	17.0	Fed of	13	2.1
Australia	160	17.0	Japan	186	2.1
Canada	249	15.5	Jordan	2	1.3
New Zealand	32	14.7	Belgium	12	1.3
Ecuador[1]	54	14.2	Laos[1]	2	1.3
Chile[2]	96	14.2	United	60	1.2
Austria	80	11.5	Czechoslova	15	1.1
Venezuela	66	11.1	Kenya	7	1.1
Brazil[1]	593	10.1	Ireland	3	1.0
Luxemburg	3	9.8	France	45	1.0
Peru	94	9.7	Thailand	17	0.8
Paraguay	15	9.3	South Africa	11	0.8
Norway	**31**	**9.0**	Netherlands	8	0.7
Mexico	227	7.3	Mozambique	4	0.7
Finland	27	6.3	South Korea	13	0.6
West Germany	294	5.8	Egypt	13	0.5
Italy	165	5.7	Syria	2	0.5
Spain	165	5.7	Ceylon	2	0.2
Haiti[1]	17	5.1	Turkey	5	0.2
Sweden	35	4.8	Nigeria[1]	4	0.1
Switzerland[2]	23	4.5	Pakistan	8	0.1
Denmark	19	4.3	India[1]	29	0.1

Source: The number of radio stations for each country is from: Statistical Office of the United Nations, Department of Economic and Social Affairs. *Statistical Yearbook 1960.* New York: Statistical Office of the United Nations, 1960. Pg. 607. The population figures utilized in order to arrive at the number of radio stations per one million inhabitants are from: Statistical Office of the United Nations, Department of Economic and Social Affairs. *Demographic Yearbook 1961.* New York: Statistical Office of the United Nations, 1961. Pg. 126–137. Previous citation is for all countries except Cuba. The population figure utilized for Cuba is that reported for the year under analysis in Banco Nacional de Cuba. *Memoria 1958–59.* Havana: Banco Nacional de Cuba, 1959. Pg. 95. Notes: [1] 1955, [2] 1957

Table 22. Inhabitants per Radio Receivers in 1957.

Country	Number of Radio Receivers	Inhabitants per Radio Receiver (units)	Country	Number of Radio Receivers (000s)	Inhabitants per Radio Receiver (units)
United States	150,000	1.1	Bolivia[2]	200	16.2
Canada	9,660	1.7	Peru	600	16.5
Sweden	2,608	2.8	South Africa	866	16.9
East Germany	5,306	3.1	Paraguay	90	18.3
Denmark	1,438	3.1	Lebanon	80	19.2
United Kingdom	14,654	3.5	Yugoslavia	890	20.2
Luxemburg	87	3.5	Hong Kong	117	22.1
Norway	985	3.5	Turkey	1,098	23.2
West Germany	14,400	3.6	Algeria	429	23.6
Iceland	45	3.7	Surinam	11	24.0
Austria	1,839	3.8	Egypt	1,000	24.2
Netherlands	2,888	3.8	Dominican Rep	100	27.0
Finland	1,121	3.9	Jordan	53	28.8
Uruguay	700	3.9	Fed of Malaya	196	32.0
Belgium	2,307	3.9	Iran[2]	500	37.5
Switzerland	1,308	3.9	Ecuador[2]	100	38.0
Australia	2,308	4.2	Nicaragua	35	38.1
New Zealand	531	4.2	Syria[2]	100	39.7
Czechoslovakia	3,150	4.2	Libya	25	46.1
France	10,198	4.3	Ceylon	180	50.9

(Continued)

Table 22. (Continued)

Country	Number of Radio Receivers	Inhabitants per Radio Receiver (units)	Country	Number of Radio Receivers (000s)	Inhabitants per Radio Receiver (units)
Cuba²	**1,100**	**5.5**	Honduras	32	55.3
Hungary	1,774	5.6	Ghana	83	57.4
Ireland	477	6.0	Albania	24	60.9
Israel	315	6.1	South Korea	320	71.2
Japan	14,591	6.2	El Salvador	30	78.3
Poland	4,005	7.1	Philippines²	300	81.7
Venezuela²	750	7.9	Iraq	80	81.7
Italy	6,084	8.0	Afghanistan²	12	108.3
Panama	120	8.1	Angola	33	135.9
Bulgaria	898	8.5	Indonesia²	600	139.2
Romania	1,499	11.9	Laos²	10	160.0
Mexico¹	2,500	12.0	Haiti¹	19	176.0
Greece	628	12.9	Mozambique	24	257.1
Brazil	4,570	13.4	Kenya	24	277.8
Costa Rica	75	13.8	Thailand	73	288.7
Spain	2,105	14.0	India	1,347	303.9
Greenland	2	14.5	Nigeria	61	544.0
Portugal	596	14.9	Cambodia²	7	622.7
Colombia²	800	16.2	Pakistan	140	624.2

Source: Statistical Office of the United Nations, Department of Economic and Social Affairs. *Statistical Yearbook 1959*. New York: Statistical Office of the United Nations, 1959. Pg. 584. For population statistics see Table 21.
Notes: [1] 1955, [2] 1956

Table 23. Cinema Attendance per Capita in the 1950s.

Country	Movie Tickets Sold per Capita (units)	Year	Country	Movie Tickets Sold per Capita (units)	Year
Australia	21.3	1958	Yugoslavia	6.2	1958
Ireland	18.8	1957	Brazil	5.7	1957
Austria	17.4	1958	Netherlands	5.7	1958
New Zealand	16.7	1958	Jamaica	4.9	1957
Israel	16.1	1958	Nicaragua	4.6	1952
Iceland	15.0	1958	El Salvador	4.5	1958
Italy	15.0	1958	South Africa	4.4	1950
United Kingdom	14.5	1958	Albania	4.4	1958
Germany West	13.8	1958	Colombia	4.1	1958
United States	12.5	1958	Argentina	3.9	1957
Japan	12.3	1958	Chile	3.8	1958
Singapore	11.7	1958	India	3.5	1958
Denmark	11.1	1958	Puerto Rico	3.4	1959
Spain	10.4	1957	Indonesia	3.0	1957
Belgium	9.9	1959	Egypt	2.9	1958
Norway	9.7	1958	Guatemala	2.9	1958
Sweden	9.4	1958	Ceylon	2.9	1958
Uruguay	9.1	1958	Portugal	2.9	1958

(Continued)

Table 23. (Continued)

Country	Movie Tickets Sold per Capita (units)	Year	Country	Movie Tickets Sold per Capita (units)	Year
Cuba	**9.0**	**1958**	Jordan	2.7	1958
France	8.8	1958	Iran	2.5	1961
Canada	8.6	1958	Ecuador	2.4	1952
Mexico	8.5	1957	Algeria	2.3	1958
Venezuela	8.2	1958	China (mainland)	2.2	1956
Switzerland	7.2	1957	Dominican Rep	2.1	1955
Finland	7.1	1958	Vietnam	1.4	1958
Poland	7.1	1958	Pakistan	1.0	1959
China (Taiwan)	6.8	1958	South Korea	0.9	1958
Peru	6.6	1958	Philippines	0.6	1958
Greece	6.3	1958	Angola	0.3	1958
Romania	6.2	1958	Haiti	0.3	1958

Source: Statistical Office of the United Nations, Department of Economic and Social Affairs. *Statistical Yearbook 1959*. New York: Statistical Office of the United Nations, 1959. Pg. 581.

Statistical Office of the United Nations, Department of Economic and Social Affairs. *Statistical Yearbook 1960*. New York: Statistical Office of the United Nations, 1960. Pg. 606.

Statistical Office of the United Nations, Department of Economic and Social Affairs. *Statistical Yearbook 1961*. New York: Statistical Office of the United Nations, 1961. Pg. 644.

Statistical Office of the United Nations, Department of Economic and Social Affairs. *Statistical Yearbook 1962*. New York: Statistical Office of the United Nations, 1962. Pg. 654.

Table 24. Newspaper Circulation in the 1950s.

Country	Number of Daily Newspapers (units)	Copies per 1000 Inhabitants (units)	Year
United Kingdom	114	573	1954
Sweden	139	462	1956
Luxemburg	5	455	1956
Finland	101	420	1956
Japan	255	397	1955
New Zealand	42	390	1956
Iceland	5	389	1957
Belgium	39	383	1952
Australia	53	381	1957
Denmark	126	376	1955
Norway	84	374	1956
United States	1824	337	1956
Switzerland	120	296	1956
Germany West	481	277	1956
Netherlands	65	264	1956
Portugal	28	61	1954
Colombia	37	60	1956
South Africa	19	57	1952
South Korea	43	55	1956
Ecuador	24	50	1952
Jamaica	2	49	1955
Mexico	162	48	1952
Yugoslavia	18	48	1956
Albania	2	45	1958
El Salvador	7	44	1957
Bolivia	6	35	1957
Turkey	116	32	1952
Ceylon	8	30	1956
Paraguay	6	28	1957
Dominican Rep	6	27	1957

(Continued)

Table 24. (Continued)

Country	Number of Daily Newspapers (units)	Copies per 1000 Inhabitants (units)	Year	Country	Number of Daily Newspapers (units)	Copies per 1000 Inhabitants (units)	Year
France	130	246	1956	Guatemala	7	26	1956
Canada	98	244	1956	Honduras	7	21	1956
Ireland	9	242	1956	Egypt	46	20	1958
Singapore	11	210	1957	Philippines	19	19	1956
Uruguay	12	200	1957	Syria	40	19	1958
Israel	24	199	1956	Jordan	4	17	1956
Austria	34	187	1956	Fed of Malaya	11	14	1956
Argentina	346	159	1956	Indonesia	95	11	1958
Cuba	**58**	**129**	**1956**	Iraq	16	10	1957
Panama	11	124	1957	China (mainland)	392	9	1956
East Germany	37	118	1954	India	465	9	1958
Italy	109	103	1958	Pakistan	80	9	1955

Country		
Venezuela	32	1956
Lebanon	46	1957
Costa Rica	5	1957
Nicaragua	10	1957
Peru	58	1957
Chile	43	1952
Greece	68	1952
Spain	101	1956
Puerto Rico	3	1955

Country			
Angola	3	6	1956
Iran	24	5	1958
Thailand	30	4	1952
Haiti	6	3	1956
Cambodia	7	3	1955
Saudi Arabia	2	2	1957
Afghanistan	2	1	1958
Ethiopia	5	0.5	1956

Sources: Statistical Office of the United Nations, Department of Economic and Social Affairs. *Statistical Yearbook 1957*. New York: Statistical Office of the United Nations, 1957. Pg. 634.
Statistical Office of the United Nations, Department of Economic and Social Affairs. *Statistical Yearbook 1958*. New York: Statistical Office of the United Nations, 1958. Pg. 571.
Statistical Office of the United Nations, Department of Economic and Social Affairs. *Statistical Yearbook 1959*. New York: Statistical Office of the United Nations, 1959. Pg. 578.
Statistical Office of the United Nations, Department of Economic and Social Affairs. *Statistical Yearbook 1960*. New York: Statistical Office of the United Nations, 1960. Pg. 602.
Statistical Office of the United Nations, Department of Economic and Social Affairs. *Statistical Yearbook 1961*. New York: Statistical Office of the United Nations, 1961. Pg. 638.
Statistical Office of the United Nations, Department of Economic and Social Affairs. *Statistical Yearbook 1962*. New York: Statistical Office of the United Nations, 1962. Pg. 649.

Table 25. Telephone Units per 100 Inhabitants in 1958.

Country	Telephones Units per 100 Inhabitants
United States	38.12
Sweden	32.50
Canada	29.99
Switzerland	28.45
New Zealand	28.10
Lebanon	27.11
Denmark	21.67
Iceland	21.46
Australia	19.68
Norway	19.08
United Kingdom	14.40
Netherlands	12.53
Finland	12.46
Belgium	11.40
West Germany	9.76
Austria	8.76
France	8.31
Italy	6.13
Argentina	6.04
Czechoslovakia	5.86
South Africa	5.51
Spain	4.98
Uruguay	4.92
Ireland	4.88
Japan	4.74
Israel	4.67
Portugal	3.70
Singapore	3.64
Puerto Rico	3.30
Cuba	**2.61**
Venezuela	2.51

Economic Participation and Standards of Living in the 1950s

Country	Telephones Units per 100 Inhabitants
Chile	2.28
Hungary	2.23
Greece	2.05
Peru	1.87
Colombia	1.83
Algeria	1.58
Poland	1.55
Brazil	1.48
Mexico	1.36
Yugoslavia	1.20
Syria	1.13
Fed. Of Malaya	1.00
Egypt	0.75
Libya	0.75
Iraq	0.67
Turkey	0.64
Ecuador	0.62
China (Taiwan)	0.59
Dominican Republic	0.59
Paraguay	0.54
Afghanistan	0.54
Nicaragua	0.51
Kenya	0.50
El Salvador	0.48
Iran	0.41
Ghana	0.39
Ceylon	0.34
Guatemala	0.33
Honduras	0.32
South Korea	0.29
Philippines	0.28
Mozambique	0.16

(Continued)

Table 25. (Continued)

Country	Telephones Units per 100 Inhabitants
Thailand	0.15
Angola	0.14
Haiti	0.12
Indonesia	0.10
Republic Viet Nam	0.10
India	0.09
Nigeria	0.09
Pakistan	0.07
Cambodia	0.06
Burma	0.05

Source: Statistical Office of the United Nations, Department of Economic and Social Affairs. *Statistical Yearbook 1960*. New York: Statistical Office of the United Nations, 1960. Pg. 600.

in the world (table 19). And, secondly, its citizens had more television sets, on a per capita basis, than every country in the world with the exception of the United States, Canada, and the United Kingdom (table 20).

The stage of development of a country's radio industry and the penetration of radio receivers among the population of a country were similarly indicative of strong capital investment in the country, of the strength of commercial activity and thus advertising, and, relatedly, of robust purchasing power prowess among a country's population. All of this for the same reasons as those just provided for the television industry, while of course noting that radio stations require less capital than television stations, and that radio receivers cost less than television receivers. Here, once again, Cuba's position in the world was nothing short of impressive. The country had one of the highest densities of radio stations in the world (table 21) and a greater penetration of radio receivers per capita than the great majority of the world's nations, including developed economies such as Japan, Italy, Greece, Spain, and Portugal (table 22). This is particularly noticeable since Cuba, as constrasting with some smaller countries, did not have as heavy of a concentration of population in its capital city.

In the 1950s, the movie theater was another leading cultural media outlet that required a high level of capital investment and widespread purchasing power to establish itself broadly. The prevalence of such a cultural outlet also has as a requisite a sufficiently educated and sophisticated populace to which it could address its then modern message. Cuba's ranking in the number of movie tickets sold per capita (table 23) was yet another clear indicator of such achievements, as the island ranked ahead of France, Canada, Switzerland, and a number of other developed nations.

Similar conclusions can be drawn from the fact that Cuba's ranking in the number of newspaper dailies and their level of circulation, as table 24 confirms, was higher than in a number of developed and highly cultured countries such as Italy, Spain, Greece, and Portugal. This would once again happen only in a country with high levels of disposable income per capita, a broad distribution of that income, and a particularly well-educated populace.

In addition to being well informed and entertained by the country's newspaper, television, radio, and movie theater infrastructure, Cubans in the 1950s were also highly connected with each other by the standards of the day. As table 25 below shows, Cuba had more telephone units installed per one hundred inhabitants in 1958 than every country in Latin America, with the exception of Argentina and Uruguay, ahead of Greece and most of the countries in Eastern Europe, and ahead of every country in Asia other than Japan and Singapore.

Notes

1. United States Department of Commerce. *Investment in Cuba: Basic Information for United States Businessmen*. Washington, DC: US Government Printing Office, 1956. Pg. 184.
2. Ibid., pg. 22.
3. *Cuban Constitution*. Article LXI, 1940.
4. Cordova, Efren. "La Nueva Tarifa General de Salario Minimos de Cuba." *Revista Cubana de Derecho*. 30.2 (1958): pg. 3.

5

Education and Health Care in the 1950s

As the decade of the 1950s came to a close, Cuba's impressive standing with respect to indicators measuring overall macroeconomic development, as well as those measuring the population's standard of living as reflected in their purchasing power and the sophistication of the goods and services that they were consuming, were coupled with other important achievements in social spheres. Particularly important were those in education and health care. These two critical components of a nation's fabric had been prioritized by Cubans in synchronicity with the country's economic development. Correspondingly, the private and public sectors had made significant investments in education and health care that led to the island attaining very advanced standings relative to most countries in both of these areas. These achievements, in addition to being critical to the quality of life that Cubans had attained at that particular point in time, also bode well for future economic growth, which is always greatly stimulated by a well-educated, healthy population. That additional economic growth would, given the country's prioritization of these two areas, in turn ensure that the virtuous cycle would continue, driving further achievement in both of these socially vital areas.

Education

In addition to highlighting the strong purchasing power and disposable income that Cubans had achieved by the decade of the 1950s, a number of the tables presented in the previous chapter also clearly pointed to Cubans having made significant educational advances and being culturally connected. Examples of this are the statistics presented with respect to television and radio penetration, cinema attendance and newspaper circulation. Without a strong educational foundation for its citizens, the island would not have developed anywhere near to the level that it did with respect to any of the aforementioned indicators,

63

or, for that matter, all of the other impressive macroeconomic metrics that are presented in this book.

Cuba's prioritization of education manifested itself in the strong public and private school system that developed on the island during its republican period. Strong private primary, secondary, and higher education centers existed throughout the island, particularly focused around religiously affiliated institutions. Even more significantly, Cuba's public budget included robust annual investments in education each year to provide free and broad access to quality educational opportunities for its population. In 1954, for example, Cuba spent 4.1 percent of its GDP in education, double the ratio spent by France, more than triple that of Spain, and higher than almost every country in the world,

Table 26. Public Expenditure in Education as % of National Income in the 1950s.

Country	% of National Income	Country	% of National Income
Czechoslovakia	6.5%	Jamaica	2.4%
East Germany	6.2%	Philippines	2.4%
Japan	6.1%	Belgium	2.4%
Hungary	5.0%	Brazil	2.3%
Puerto Rico	4.8%	Peru	2.3%
Poland	4.8%	Venezuela	2.3%
South Africa	4.1%	Syria	2.3%
Cuba	**4.1%**	Cambodia	2.0%
United States	4.0%	France	2.0%
Austria	4.0%	Guatemala	1.8%
Panama	3.8%	Chile	1.8%
Denmark	3.8%	Colombia	1.8%
Ireland	3.5%	Australia	1.8%
New Zealand	3.5%	Luxemburg	1.7%
Canada	3.2%	USRR	1.7%
Argentina	3.2%	Dominican Rep	1.6%
Norway	3.2%	Hong Kong	1.5%
United Kingdom	3.2%	Turkey	1.5%
China	3.1%	Portugal	1.4%
Finland	3.1%	Congo	1.3%
Algeria	3.0%	Ecuador	1.3%
Israel	3.0%	Paraguay	1.3%

Country	% of National Income	Country	% of National Income
West Germany	3.0%	Greece	1.3%
Iceland	3.0%	Indonesia	1.2%
El Salvador	2.9%	Lebanon	1.2%
Netherlands	2.9%	Spain	1.2%
Ghana	2.8%	Yugoslavia	1.2%
Iraq	2.8%	Haiti	1.0%
Bulgaria	2.8%	Honduras	1.0%
Italy	2.7%	Mexico	1.0%
Switzerland	2.7%	India	0.8%
Costa Rica	2.6%	Thailand	0.6%
Sweden	2.6%	Pakistan	0.5%
Kenya	2.5%	South Korea	0.1%

Source: United Nations, Educational, Scientific and Cultural Organization (UNESCO). Statistical Yearbook 1963. Paris: UNESCO, 1963. Pg. 282.

Table 27. Percentage of Public Expenditure on Education in 1958.

Country	% of Public Expenditure in Education
Cuba	**23.0%**
Puerto Rico	21.5%
Argentina	19.6%
Costa Rica	19.6%
Chile	15.7%
Pure	14.6%
Mexico	14.7%
Guatemala	11.7%
Ecuador	10.8%

Source: United Nations, Educational, Scientific and Cultural Organization (UNESCO). *Annuaire International De L'éducation*. Paris: UNESCO, 1959.

including the United States (table 26). In 1958, expenditures in education accounted for 23 percent of total Cuban public expenditures, making it the second most important public expenditure category in the country, following health care, and representing a higher proportion of total public expenditure than what was spent in most of the world (table 27).[1]

This level of expenditure ensured Cubans with broad access to practically free schooling from kindergarten through university, including the University of Havana, which was the country's best. At the primary school level, for example, Cuba's expenditures on education afforded the island's population with a higher ratio of teachers per one thousand inhabitants than a number of developed countries, including the UK, Portugal, and Spain (table 28).

Table 28. Primary Teachers per 1,000 Inhabitants in the 1950s.

Country	Primary Teachers per 1000 Inhabitants	Year	Country	Primary Teachers per 1000 Inhabitants	Year
Canada	8.1	1954–57	Luxembourg	3.6	1957
Costa Rica	6.5	1957	Puerto Rico	3.6	1954–57
Israel	6.1	1955–56	**Cuba**	**3.4**	**1956**
Sweden	5.7	1954–56	Venezuela	3.3	1957
Argentina	5.6	1954–56	United Kingdom	3.0	1956–57
Iceland	5.5	1954–56	Peru	3.0	1955–1956
Czechoslovakia	5.3	1956	Nicaragua	2.9	1953–56
Denmark	5.3	1955–56	El Salvador	2.9	1956
Finland	5.2	1956–57	Ecuador	2.9	1955–56
Bulgaria	5.2	1956–57	Mexico	2.7	1955–1956
Romania	5.1	1957	Portugal	2.65	1956
Jordan	5.0	1955–56	Uruguay	2.64	1955–57
New Zealand	4.9	1956–57	Colombia	2.62	1956
Singapore	4.7	1955–1956	Honduras	2.61	1954–1957
Ireland	4.6	1956	Brazil	2.58	1954–55
Norway	4.4	1954–56	China	2.6	1955–56
Thailand	4.4	1956–57	Guatemala	2.5	1956
United States	4.3	1955–57	Afghanistan	2.5	1954–56
Panama	4.3	1954–1956	Yugoslavia	2.3	1956
South Africa	4.1	1955–1957	Spain	2.3	1954–56
Albania	4.0	1954–56	Egypt	2.3	1957
Netherlands	4.0	1957	Bolivia	2.1	1956
Japan	3.9	1957	Turkey	1.9	1956–57

Country	Primary Teachers per 1000 Inhabitants	Year	Country	Primary Teachers per 1000 Inhabitants	Year
Philippines	3.7	1955–57	Iraq	1.9	1956
Germany West	3.7	1956–57	India	1.7	1955–56
Italy	3.7	1955–56	Haiti	1.3	1955–56
Chile	3.6	1954–56	Angola	0.8	1957
Austria	3.6	1957			

Source: Number of Teachers for Cuba is from: Statistical Office of the United Nations, Department of Economic and Social Affairs. *Statistical Yearbook 1960*. New York: Statistical Office of the United Nations, 1960. Pg. 574. The figures for all other countries are from: Statistical Office of the United Nations, Department of Economic and Social Affairs. *Statistical Yearbook 1958*. New York: Statistical Office of the United Nations, 1958. Pg. 545. Also, Statistical Office of the United Nations, Department of Economic and Social Affairs. *Statistical Yearbook 1959*. New York: Statistical Office of the United Nations, 1959. Pg. 552.

Table 29. Libraries per Million Inhabitants in the 1950s.

Country	Libraries per Million
Argentina	123
Panama	98
Cuba	**88**
Chile	64
Peru	53
Honduras	38
Brazil	35
Guatemala	25
Colombia	22

Source: Panamerican Union. *América en Cifras 1960*. 2.82. Washington, DC: Panamerican Union, 1960. Pg. 15.

In addition, Cuba's prioritization of education was also evident in the number of libraries that dotted the island. As table 29 highlights, Cuba had more libraries per million inhabitants than most other Latin American nations.

All of these positive factors with respect to the island's emphasis on education translated into a very broad proportion (within the context of the times) of Cuba's population being literate. As table 30

Table 30. Literacy Rates, 1946–1960.

Country	Literacy Rate	Year	Country	Literacy Rate	Year
Japan	97.8	1960	Paraguay	65.8	1950
United States	96.8	1950	Colombia	62.3	1951
Belgium	96.7	1947	Philippines	60.0	1948
France	96.4	1946	Mexico	56.8	1950
Hungary	95.3	1949	Portugal	55.9	1950
Poland	93.8	1950	Ecuador	55.7	1950
Israel	93.7	1948	Venezuela	52.2	1950
Romania	88.6	1956	Thailand	52.0	1947
Argentina	86.4	1947	China	50.1	1950
Italy	85.9	1951	Singapore	49.8	1957
Bulgaria	85.3	1956	Brazil	49.4	1950
Spain	82.4	1950	Dominican Republic	42.9	1950
Chile	80.2	1952	El Salvador	40.4	1950
Costa Rica	79.4	1950	Nicaragua	38.4	1950
Cuba	**77.9**	**1953**	Honduras	35.2	1950
South Korea	76.8	1955	Guatemala	34.4	1950
Greece	74.1	1951	Bolivia	32.1	1950
Puerto Rico	73.3	1950	Turkey	31.9	1950
Yugoslavia	72.7	1953	South Africa	27.5	1946
Albania	71.7	1955	India	19.3	1951
Hong Kong	71.4	1961	Morocco	13.8	1960
Panama	69.9	1950	Haiti	10.5	1950

Source: United Nations, Educational, Scientific and Cultural Organization (UNESCO). *Statistical Yearbook 1963*. Paris: UNESCO, 1963. Pg. 27.

summarizes, Cuba's literacy rate in the 1950s was, in fact, equivalent to that of the Greeks, higher than Portugal's and more than double that of Turkey's. Moreover, it was higher than that of every country in Latin America except Costa Rica, Chile, and Argentina. Furthermore, the island's level of literacy was continuing to increase rapidly, with a focus on expanding the penetration of schools in rural areas, where literacy was the lowest, as was of course also the case in all other countries of the world.

Importantly, Cuba's high literacy rate and the availability of educational opportunities translated into significant levels of participation in higher education. As table 31 shows, Cuba's ratio of higher education students per one thousand inhabitants was, in fact, one of the highest in the world, ahead of Japan, France, Italy, Germany, and England. This was a critical element that ensured that the island's human capital was sufficiently educated and skilled to drive ongoing improvements in Cuba's productivity and standards of living.

Lastly, the composition of the Cuban student body also revealed how socially advanced the island had become, as the percentage of Cuban students that were female, 45 percent, was the highest in the Americas and one of the highest in the world in 1958 (table 32).

Table 31. Higher Education Students per 1,000 Inhabitants in 1957–1958.

Country	Higher Education Students per 1,000
United States	17.7
Cuba	**13.5**
USSR	9.5
Japan	6.9
France	4.1
Italy	3.2
Germany	3.0
England	1.9

Source: United Nations, Educational, Scientific and Cultural Organization (UNESCO). *Annuaire International De L'éducation.* Paris: UNESCO, 1959.

Table 32. Percentage of Female Students to Total Enrolled in the 1950s.

Country	% of Female Students to Total Students Enrolled	Year	Country	% of Female Students to Total Students Enrolled	Year
Cuba	**45%**	1955	Nicaragua	24%	1959
Panama	45%	1955	Israel	24%	1950
Puerto Rico	45%	1955	Dominican Republic	24%	1955
Costa Rica	42%	1955	Greece	24%	1955

(Continued)

Table 32. (Continued)

Country	% of Female Students to Total Students Enrolled	Year	Country	% of Female Students to Total Students Enrolled	Year
Finland	42%	1955	Hungary	24%	1955
Chile	39%	1955	Peru	22%	1955
United Kingdom	37%	1955	Ecuador	20%	1955
Romania	35%	1955	Austria	20%	1955
United States	34%	1955	Luxembourg	20%	1955
Bulgaria	33%	1950	El Salvador	19%	1955
Hong Kong	31%	1955	West Germany	19%	1955
Czechoslovakia	31%	1959	Albania	18%	1955
Yugoslavia	31%	1955	Norway	18%	1955
France	30%	1955	Poland	18%	1955
Canada	29%	1955	Spain	18%	1955
Paraguay	29%	1950	Colombia	17%	1955
Denmark	29%	1955	Turkey	17%	1955
East Germany	29%	1955	Japan	16%	1955
Ireland	29%	1955	Belgium	16%	1950
Sweden	29%	1955	Taiwan	15%	1955
Italy	28%	1955	Switzerland	15%	1955
Australia	28%	1955	India	14%	1955
Argentina	27%	1955	South Korea	11%	1955
Portugal	27%	1955	Iran	9%	1955
Venezuela	25%	1955	Honduras	7%	1954
Netherlands	25%	1955			

Source: United Nations, Educational, Scientific and Cultural Organization (UNESCO). *Statistical Yearbook 1963*. Paris: UNESCO, 1963. Pg. 210.

All of these elements combined to create a literate, progressive, and culturally connected society that was active and competitive in the world stage and was well-positioned to continue to advance Cuba both socially and economically.

Health Care

Similar to education, Cuban emphasis on health care goes back to the island's republican period. During that period, an advanced public and private health care system provided the country with access to well-equipped hospitals and clinics. These included a combination of private networks, such as Clínica Sagrado Corazón, Clínica Antonetti, Clínica Miramar, Clínica Marfan, Centro Médico-Quirúrgico, and the quintas, such as Quinta de Asociación de Dependientes del Comercio and Quinta Canaria, which were priced to be very accessible to a large proportion of the island's population and provided the framework for the establishment of the first US Healthcare Maintenance Organization (HMO) in Miami in the 1970s. Additionally, for those that could not afford the cost of the private clinics, a vast network of free first-aid facilities clinics was available throughout Cuba, known as the Casas de Socorro. The Casas de Socorro were tasked with providing quality basic health care and triage, and, in the event that more involved procedures were necessary, patients would be referred for free care to one of the island's many public hospitals, which comprised the majority of the country's major hospitals (fifty-four of the seventy-nine major hospitals throughout the island were public), and which were also some of the most prestigious, such as Calixto García Hospital, Reina Mercedes Hospital, and Curie Hospital. This network of clinics and hospitals was well staffed by highly trained physicians to a level that placed Cuba in a leading position among the countries of the world in terms of the number of physicians available to the island's population. As table 33 shows, Cuba had more physicians available per one thousand inhabitants than Norway, Ireland, Spain, Sweden, the UK, Portugal, and Finland.

This level of access to quality health care allowed Cuba to have, at the end of the 1950s, one of the lowest total mortality and infant mortality rates in the world. In fact, Cuba's overall mortality rate was the third lowest reported worldwide (table 34).

Part of any nation's ranking with respect to its total mortality rate is driven by the age distribution of that country's population in addition to the quality of its health care and access to quality nutrition. Cuba's total mortality standing points to a population that was both younger and healthier than most of the world. These two conditions, in addition to being positive from a purely social perspective, also had important positive implications for the island's prospective macroeconomic growth.

71

Table 33. Physicians per 1,000 Inhabitants in the 1950s.

Country	Physicians per 1,000 Inhabitants	Year	Country	Physicians per 1,000 Inhabitants	Year
Israel	2.23	1957	Surinam	0.56	1957
USSR	1.81	1957	South Africa	0.51	1956
Czechoslovakia	1.63	1958	Chile	0.51	1959
Austria	1.50	1958	Paraguay	0.51	1958
Italy	1.45	1956	Singapore	0.45	1957
Switzerland	1.37	1958	China (Taiwan)	0.44	1956
West Germany	1.36	1958	Peru	0.44	1957
Bulgaria	1.33	1958	Turkey	0.43	1959
Argentina	1.31	1956	Brazil	0.41	1954
United States	1.29	1956	Panama	0.37	1957
New Zealand	1.23	1958	Costa Rica	0.37	1957
Belgium	1.22	1958	Nicaragua	0.36	1956
Romania	1.21	1958	Egypt	0.34	1957
Denmark	1.20	1957	Colombia	0.34	1957
Greece	1.19	1958	Ecuador	0.34	1957
Australia	1.17	1956	Jamaica	0.26	1957
Iceland	1.16	1955	Bolivia	0.26	1957
Uruguay	1.13	1958	Iran	0.22	1958
Canada	1.08	1958	Ceylon	0.21	1958
France	1.06	1957	Dominican Republic	0.21	1956
Netherlands	1.06	1957	Honduras	0.21	1957
Japan	1.05	1957	India	0.19	1956
Luxembourg	1.04	1957	Albania	0.19	1957
Cuba	**1.01**	**1957**	El Salvador	0.19	1957
Norway	1.00	1957	Algeria	0.18	1958
Ireland	0.99	1951	Iraq	0.18	1958
Spain	0.94	1958	Afghanistan	0.17	1957
Lebanon	0.86	1957	Guatemala	0.16	1957
Sweden	0.85	1957	Jordan	0.15	1958

Country	Physicians per 1,000 Inhabitants	Year	Country	Physicians per 1,000 Inhabitants	Year
Poland	0.85	1958	Thailand	0.15	1957
United Kingdom	0.82	1957	Libya	0.13	1957
Portugal	0.74	1957	Philippines	0.10	1958
Puerto Rico	0.69	1958	Pakistan	0.06	1958
Finland	0.59	1957	Angola	0.05	1958
Venezuela	0.58	1958	Haiti	0.04	1957
Yugoslavia	0.58	1956	Nigeria	0.02	1958
Mexico	0.57	1957	Cambodia	0.00	1958

Source: Statistical Office of the United Nations, Department of Economic and Social Affairs. *Statistical Yearbook 1961*. New York: Statistical Office of the United Nations, 1961. Pg. 607. The population figure used for Cuba to arrive at the metric per inhabitant is from: Banco Nacional de Cuba. *Memoria 1958–59*. Havana: Banco Nacional de Cuba, 1959. Pg. 95. Population for all of the other countries was obtained from: Statistical Office of the United Nations, Department of Economic and Social Affairs. *Demographic Yearbook 1961*. New York: Statistical Office of the United Nations, 1961. Pg. 126.

Table 34. Mortality Rates per 1,000 Inhabitants in 1956.

Country	Mortality Rate Per 1,000 Inhabitants	Country	Mortality Rate Per 1,000 Inhabitants
Iraq	3.8	Finland	9.0
Lebanon	5.5	Australia	9.1
Cuba	**5.8**	Dominican Republic	9.1
Israel	6.6	Panama	9.2
Uruguay	7.0	United States	9.3
Iceland	7.2	Bulgaria	9.4
Puerto Rico	7.3	Costa Rica	9.6
Greece	7.4	Sweden	9.6
Singapore	7.5	Czechoslovakia	9.6
Viet-Nam	7.5	Romania	9.9
USSR	7.6	Spain	9.9
Iran	7.7	Venezuela	10.0

(Continued)

Table 34. (Continued)

Country	Mortality Rate Per 1,000 Inhabitants	Country	Mortality Rate Per 1,000 Inhabitants
Netherlands	7.8	Bolivia	10.0
Taiwan	8.0	Switzerland	10.2
Japan	8.0	Italy	10.3
Nicaragua	8.1	Hungry	10.5
Canada	8.2	China	11.4
Argentina	8.2	Ireland	11.7
Jordan	8.3	Chile	12.1
Norway	8.7	Peru	12.1
Denmark	8.9	Portugal	12.1
Liechtenstein	8.9	Belgium	12.2
Poland	9.0	France	12.5
New Zealand	9.0	Colombia	13.3
Philippines	9.0	Ecuador	14.8

Source: Statistical Office of the United Nations, Department of Economic and Social Affairs. *Demographic Yearbook 1960*. New York: Statistical Office of the United Nations, 1960. Pg. 498.

When one examines the world's life expectancy levels, which more directly isolate the impact of a population's access to quality health care and nutrition, a very favorable picture also emerges for Cuba. As table 35 shows, Cuba's ranking with respect to life expectancy was higher than that of Portugal's and Turkey's in Europe, as well as a long list of other countries, including every country in Latin America, with the exception of Argentina, whose population had a life expectancy that was just slightly over two years more than Cuba's. Cuba's ranking was also more than 12 years higher, or over 26 percent greater, than the world average of 49.4 years for that period of time.

Cuba's ranking with respect to infant mortality was even more impressive. As can be seen in table 36, as of 1949, the closest year to 1959 for which international bodies reported data for Cuba, the island ranked behind a very short list of countries, and ahead of developed nations such as Canada, Belgium, West Germany, France, Italy, and Spain, among many others.

Table 35. Life Expectancy at Birth (1955–1960).

Country	Life Expectancy (Years)
Norway	73.5
Netherlands	72.9
Sweden	72.8
Denmark	72.1
Switzerland	70.7
New Zealand	70.6
Australia	70.5
United Kingdom	70.5
Canada	70.2
United States of America	69.6
Belgium	69.4
Czech Republic	69.4
France	69.2
Ireland	69.0
Germany	68.9
Cyprus	68.7
Italy	68.4
Finland	68.0
Austria	67.9
Luxembourg	67.5
Spain	67.5
Greece	67.2
Bulgaria	66.3
Japan	66.3
Hong Kong	66.0
Poland	65.9
Russian Federation	64.8
Argentina	64.5
Singapore	64.0
Croatia	63.6
Jamaica	62.6
Lebanon	62.4
Cuba	**62.3**
Portugal	61.8
Costa Rica	60.1

(Continued)

Table 35. (Continued)

Country	Life Expectancy (Years)
Panama	59.5
Venezuela	58.1
Malaysia	57.9
Viet Nam	57.3
Philippines	57.1
Chile	56.2
Mexico	55.3
Colombia	55.2
Brazil	53.5
Ecuador	51.4
South Korea	51.2
North Korea	49.9
Dominican Republic	49.9
Botswana	49.7
World	49.4
El Salvador	49.3
South Africa	48.0
Sudan	47.1
Congo	46.8
Egypt	46.4
Peru	46.3
China	45.0
Ghana	44.7
Turkey	43.7
Iran	43.5
Indonesia	42.7
Bolivia	41.9
Myanmar	41.2
Cambodia	41.0
Cameroon	40.5
Democratic Republic of the Congo	40.5
India	39.6
Papua New Guinea	37.2
Nigeria	36.0

Source: United Nations, Department of Economic and Social Affairs, Population Division; World Population Prospects: The 2012 Revision; Life Expectancy at Birth; United Nations Population Division, 2012; Web; Mar. 2014.

Table 36. Infant Mortality Rates in 1949.

Country	Infant Mortality Rate (per 1,000 Live Births)	Country	Infant Mortality Rate (per 1,000 Live Births)
Sweden	23.3	Panama	70.7
Iceland	23.7	Japan	62.5
Australia	25.3	Argentina	67.0
Netherlands	26.8	Thailand	68.2
Norway	27.7	Italy	73.9
Liechtenstein	28.9	Spain	74.6
New Zealand	30.0	Austria	75.2
United States	31.3	Puerto Rico	78.3
United Kingdom	34.1	Surinam	78.6
Switzerland	34.3	Dominican Republic	81.3
Denmark	34.5	Czechoslovakia	82.4
Cuba	**37.6**	Venezuela	90.7
Canada	43.3	Honduras	92.7
Luxemburg	45.7	Guatemala	101.7
Taiwan	47.9	Peru	105.2
Finland	48.3	Mexico	106.4
Israel	51.5	Ecuador	115.2
Ireland	53.2	Costa Rica	119.6
Belgium	57.2	Nicaragua	123.3
West Germany	58.4	Colombia	134.1
France	60.2	Chile	155.2

Source: The data for all of the countries except Cuba comes from: Statistical Office of the United Nations, Department of Economic and Social Affairs. *Demographic Yearbook 1955*. New York: Statistical Office of the United Nations, 1955. Pg. 700–707. Cuba's data is from: United States Bureau of the Census. *Statistical Abstract of the United States 1960*. Ed. 81. Washington, DC: United States Department of Commerce, 1961. Pg. 921.
Note: 1949 is chosen as the year of comparison because it is the latest available figure published before 1959 for Cuba in the aforementioned sources.

Note

1.   The year used to highlight the proportion of GDP that was spent in education is different from the year used to highlight the proportion of public expenditures that went toward education because the data was not available in the source publications for the same years prior to 1959.

6

Prospects for Future Growth

In his seminal book, *The Stages of Economic Growth*,[1] late MIT professor of economics Walt Whitman Rostow defines five hierarchical stages of economic development: (i) traditional society; (ii) transitional stage: the preconditions for take-off; (iii) take-off; (iv) drive to maturity and (v) the age of high mass consumption. The most critical of the five stages is the take-off stage, where "growth becomes a country's normal condition" and eventually leads the country to stages four and five, where it achieves ongoing and self-sustaining wealth creation, higher levels of consumption and standards of living.[2]

As Professor Rostow described, for a county to enter and be in a state of developmental take-off requires that three critical conditions be met: (i) there must be "a rise in the rate of productive investment from say 5 percent or less to over 10% of national income"; (ii) a country must see "the development of one or more substantial manufacturing sectors, with a high rate of growth"; and (iii) there must be an "existence or quick emergence of a political, social and institutional framework which exploits the impulses to expansion in the modern sector and the potential external economy effects of the take-off and gives to growth an on-going character."[3] This chapter will show that Cuba had amply met all three of Rostow's conditions for take-off before the Revolution arrived. In fact, the island had solidly entered its take-off stage coincident with the early days of World War II and the signing of Cuba's 1940 Constitution. This is why, by the dawn of 1959, Cuba's socioeconomic conditions was already beginning to transition toward Rostow's fourth stage of development, the drive to maturity, and why, correspondingly, a number of the metrics previously presented in this book show Cuba's world standing as commensurate with that of countries that were in that stage of economic development and, in some cases, even in stage five.

Condition I: Productive Investment

A country's capital stock is defined as the net total value of its long-term assets, including private and public, sectorial, and social overhead. A country experiences net capital formation when the total value of its non-amortized and depreciated capital stock increases as a result of resources that are spent by corporations, private entities, parastatals, and government bodies. This results in an increase in the capital stock of the nation after accounting for depreciation and amortization. *Ceteris paribus*, the greater the physical capital that a country has per worker (capital deepening), the more that country can produce per capita. In other words, the better equipped that a labor force is, the more that said labor force can produce with the same amount of effort and ability. Given the different sizes of the population and economies of various countries, the absolute value of a country's capital investment tells little about its ranking vis-à-vis other countries. Therefore, the more useful indicator to analyze whether a country's productive investment level is adequate to bring about development is the percentage of national income that said country's net capital investment represents. In general, countries that have exhibited lasting developmental problems have suffered from low rates of net capital investment relative to their national income—generally below 5 percent. Typically, the rates of investment of stagnant countries are only enough to compensate for the rate of depreciation and amortization of the country's existing capital stock, or, when above that, not sufficient to keep up with the rate of growth of the population, or just at the pace to keep up with it. When these cases occur, the increase in output realized does not bring about improvements in the standard of living of the country.

On the other hand, countries that are in developmental stages characterized by strong endogenous economic growth (e.g., Rostow's take-off stage) typically exhibit rates of capital investment that are 10 percent or more of national income. As table 37 highlights, Cuba's capital investment as a percent of national income was nearly double this 10 percent benchmark. Cuba's 18 percent placed it alongside some of the most developed countries in the world, including the United States, France, West Germany, and the United Kingdom.

In *Stages of Economic Growth*, Professor Rostow highlights that, historically, both foreign and domestic investments have played key roles in the take-off of what eventually became developed economies.

Table 37. Capital Investment as a Percentage of GNP in 1957.

Country	Capital Investments as a % of GNP	Country	Capital Investments as a % of GNP
Switzerland	25	Belgium	17
New Zealand	23	Denmark	17
Austria	22	Greece	15
West Germany	22	Portugal	15
Italy	22	United Kingdom	15
Sweden	20	Ireland	14
France	19	United States	14
Cuba	**18**	Chile	11

Source: Statistical Office of the United Nations, Department of Economic and Social Affairs. Statistical Yearbook 1960. New York: Statistical Office of the United Nations, 1960. Pg. 471.

He points out that foreign capital was crucial in the take-off of the United States, Canada, and Sweden, while, on the other hand, the take-off stages of Japan and Britain were primarily financed with domestic capital. In Cuba, as the 1950s came to a close, both foreign and domestic capital sources were driving investment and growth. Cuba's savings rate was about 11 percent of total income in the years just before 1959, a rate that was at par with the United States, at a time when savings in the United States was at high levels.[4] At the same time, the prospects for profitability in Cuba had attracted important amounts of capital from the United States, which, as table 37 shows, had more capital invested in Cuba than in any other country of the world with the exception of Brazil, Venezuela, the UK, and Canada. When one adjusts for the size of the population of these countries, Canada and Venezuela were the only two countries in the world that attracted more US capital on a per capita basis, the latter being explained by the special case of oil investments.

The accumulation of capital driven by both domestic savings and foreign direct investment (FDI) was evident throughout all sectors of the Cuban economy. Importantly, from the perspective of supporting future growth, Cuba's strong capital investment track record was particularly evident in the quality of the country's infrastructure. In the previously mentioned *Investment in Cuba* publication, the US Department of Commerce highlighted Cuba's

Table 38. US Private Investments in 1957.

Country	Total Value of Private Investments (millions of USD)	Country	Total Value of Private Investments (millions of USD)
Canada	12,000	Honduras	110
United Kingdom[1]	2,800	Costa Rica	90
Venezuela	2,650	Pakistan	90
Brazil	1,200	Switzerland	90
Cuba	**950**	Uruguay	90
Saudi Arabia	900	Thailand	88
Mexico	800	Taiwan	80
Chile	795	Egypt	60
Argentina	700	Lebanon	55
West Germany	600	Ceylon	47
France	575	Burma	45
Philippines	475	New Zealand	45
Australia	450	Norway	45
Italy	450	El Salvador	37
Peru	400	Portugal	35
Colombia	300	Ecuador	30
Liberia	275	Haiti	25
Netherlands	220	Denmark	24
Spain	210	Nicaragua	24
Japan	190	Syria	20
Sweden	180	Indonesia	18
Guatemala	175	Greece	15
Dominican Republic	160	Libya	15
Belgium	150	Bolivia	10
India	150		

Source: Pick Publishing Corporation. *Pick's Currency Yearbook 1957*. New York: Pick Publishing Corporation, 1957. Pg. 27–338.
[1] From: Pick Publishing Corporation. *Pick's Currency Yearbook 1959*. New York: Pick Publishing Corporation, 1959. Pg. 355. Refers to statistic at the end of 1958. The datum was not available in the 1957 yearbook.

infrastructure as one of its most important attributes in support of investing in the country:

- "Few countries in the world are served better by railroads than Cuba."[5]
- "By 1955 all but 5 towns of over 5,000 in population had been connected to the republic's all-weather highway system."[6]
- "Motorized transport has become one of the leading industries of Cuba."[7]
- "Bus service on the Central Highway is excellent. Deluxe service with the latest air-conditioning equipment is featured by 3 companies, 2 of them having the double-deck, panoramic type of bus in operation. . . . [S]chedules are so frequent that there is no need to plan itineraries ahead."[8]
- "Cuba has excellent maritime services. Some 30 shipping lines operate in the Cuban trade, handling approximately 10 million metric tons of cargo annually."[9]
- "Cuba's strategic location has made its capital city, Havana, one of the most important air transport crossroads in the Western Hemisphere. . . . Havana was one of the earlier international airport terminals; the first section of what was to become the Pan American Airways System, Key West-Havana, was inaugurated in 1927."[10]

Lastly, another important example of the strength of the country's infrastructure can be seen in table 39 below, which shows that Cuba's electrification, as measured by the country's electric consumption per capita, was higher than that of Italy, Japan, Spain, Greece, and Portugal, among many others.

Table 39. Energy Consumption per Capita in 1958.

Country	Consumption per Capita (Kgs of Coal Equivalent)	Country	Consumption per Capita (Kgs of Coal Equivalent)
United States	7,640	Panama	455
Canada	5,187	Colombia	450
United Kingdom	4,741	Jamaica	437
Czechoslovakia	4,682	Hong Kong	416
East Germany	4,313	Greece	414
Belgium	3,762	Iraq	389
West Germany	3,438	Portugal	346
Sweden	2,971	Brazil	334
USSR	2,891	Peru	311
Poland	2,844	Costa Rica	260

(Continued)

Table 39. (Continued)

Country	Consumption per Capita (Kgs of Coal Equivalent)	Country	Consumption per Capita (Kgs of Coal Equivalent)
South Africa	2,616	Egypt	248
Venezuela	2,550	Turkey	246
Denmark	2,486	Algeria	237
Netherlands	2,448	Syria	225
France	2,420	Libya	209
Norway	2,380	Iran	202
Hungary	2,065	South Korea	195
Austria	1,929	Dominican Republic	191
Switzerland	1,673	Ecuador	150
Finland	1,366	Philippines	144
Romania	1,177	Jordan	142
Argentina	1,140	Guatemala	140
Israel	1,127	Bolivia	137
Ireland	1,120	India	137
Bulgaria	1,000	Nicaragua	129
Cuba	**937**	El Salvador	124
Italy	907	Honduras	120
Japan	869	Mozambique	114
Chile	799	Paraguay	84
Mexico	755	Macau	81
Spain	712	Pakistan	60
Yugoslavia	699	Angola	60
Uruguay	665	Thailand	56
Lebanon	501	Haiti	29
Taiwan	459	Laos	21

Source: Statistical Office of the United Nations, Department of Economic and Social Affairs. *Statistical Yearbook 1959*. New York: Statistical Office of the United Nations, 1959. Pg. 306.

Condition II: Industrial Growth

Consistent with Rostow's second condition for take-off, Cuba saw significant growth in not one but several of its industrial sectors during its republican period. It also saw a significant shift in the ownership of productive capacity across broad economic sectors. In a clear example of healthy economic development, foreign direct investment led to the more rapid expansion of various industries than what would have been possible based solely on domestic capital, and then, eventually, domestic owners took over these industries and moved them forward to even greater growth.

Sugar, Cuba's main export and largest contributor to GDP, was a good example of foreign-led vibrant industrial growth that was followed by a shift toward greater domestic ownership of productive activity. The 1950s saw record levels of sugar production on the island, in large part as a result of this process and the increased industrialization of the sector. The increased mechanization of sugar cane processing and the increasingly sophisticated bio-refinery activities on the island led to 125,000, or 26.3 percent, of the total 475,000 employees that were involved in the sugar industry, to be exclusively involved in the industrial side of production.[11] This level of industrialization allowed Cuba to further solidify its position as not only the largest exporter of sugar in the world, but also the world's most efficient producer, with higher industrial yields than any other country.

At the same time, the island's productive capacity increasingly became more national, as private Cuban capital bought out foreign owners. As table 40 shows, by 1958, 62 percent of Cuban sugar production was domestically owned, up nearly 40 percentage points from just twenty years earlier.

This increased level of domestic ownership meant that more of the returns from Cuba's sugar industry successes were being redeployed on the island. In this way, its lucrative position in sugar production drove a

Table 40. Evolution of Ownership of Sugar Mills.

Year	Cuban Owned		United States Owned		Owned by Others	
	#	% of total	#	% of total	#	% of total
1939	56	22%	66	55%	52	23%
1954	116	58%	41	41%	4	1%
1956	117	58%	40	41%	4	1%
1958	121	62%	36	37%	4	<1%

Source: Panamerican Union. *América en Cifras 1960*. Washington, DC: Panamerican Union, 1960.

virtuous cycle of further investments in sugar-related industrial activity and also, more importantly from a diversification point of view, in *nonsugar* industrial activity and service-oriented commercial activity, particularly in the financial sector. For example, a significant portion of the mechanization of the industry was being undertaken with machinery made in Cuba, which created a positive rippling effect that drove greater growth in domestic equipment manufacturing. Additionally, the industrialization of agriculture also went beyond sugar. This allowed the island to take advantage of one of its finest resources: its land. The quantity and quality of land available for cultivation as a proportion of the country's total land area ranked Cuba among the best agricultural nations in the world. This combination of plentiful fertile land and increased industrialization led to Cuba achieving one of the highest growths rates in post-World War II agricultural production in the world.[12] As a result, Cuba became not only self-sufficient with respect to most of its food supplies, but actually became an important exporter of foodstuffs.

Beyond the expansion of agricultural-related industrial activity, major expansions took place in other industrial sectors, such as construction, mining and oil. The construction industry experienced significant booms driven both by privately funded residential and commercial endeavors as well as social projects. These included, among other things, the building of three new highways and the development of two tunnels in Havana, which were to undergird the city's expansion. With respect to mining, the production of nickel, cobalt, copper, and magnesium grew to such an extent that Cuba reached leading world rankings in the production of all four of these minerals. In addition, new oil refineries were built and existing ones were expanded.

Also, as previously mentioned, broader sectors of Cuban commerce were also prospering. Key among these was the island's banking sector, which saw deposits grow at a rate of approximately 5 percent per year from the early 1916 to 1955.[13] The growth and increased sophistication of the banking sector on the island was so significant that, by the end of the 1950s, the largest private Latin American bank, with a world rank of 232, was the Cuban-owned Cuban Trust Co.,[14] a rather significant feat when one remembers that Cuba's population was only a small fraction of those in the largest countries in Latin America. As yet another sign of the growing independence and positive evolution of the Cuban economy during the latter part of its republican period, just like had been the case in the sugar industry, ownership of Cuba's

Table 41. National Income by Economic Activity in Latin America in 1958.

Country	Agriculture, and Fishing	Mining	Manufacturing	Construction	Electricity and Gas	Commerce, Transport, and Services	Others
Cuba	23%	1%	22%	4%	1%	43%	6%
Argentina	22%	1%	22%	4%	1%	27%	23%
Brazil	27%	–	25%	–	–	21%	27%
Chile	13%	5%	23%	3%	1%	26%	29%
Colombia	36%	4%	16%	4%	1%	19%	20%
Mexico	19%	4%	21%	2%	1%	40%	13%
Peru	24%	12%	17%	–	6%	16%	25%
Venezuela	6%	31%	12%	7%	1%	19%	24%

Source: Statistical Office of the United Nations, Department of Economic and Social Affairs. *Statistical Yearbook 1960*. New York: Statistical Office of the United Nations, 1960. Pg. 460.

banking sector also consolidated into the hands of the domestic population. Shortly before World War II, only 17 percent of the country's total deposits were held in Cuban banks. By 1955, this figure had increased to 60 percent.[15]

All this growth in industry and commerce was reflected in Cuba's economy becoming increasingly diversified. In the Annual Report (*Memoria*) of the Cuban Central Bank (the Banco Nacional de Cuba) for the year 1954, its president noted the continued increases in product per capita that were taking place in Cuba, in spite of decreasing levels of sugar production, attributing them to important expansions in the other sectors of the economy.[16] The contribution of sugar production to Cuba's gross national product, which by the beginning of the 1950s had fallen to the mid–30 percent level from much higher levels during the colonial days, fell even further during the decade of the 1950s and accounted for only 23 percent of GNP by 1958.[17]

Indeed, as table 41 shows, by 1958, among the most important economies in Latin America, Cuba had the highest percentage of national income derived from the combination of manufacturing, commerce, transport, and services. This, it should be underlined, occurred in the backdrop of strong competition from American imports, which exerted their greatest regional industrial competitive pressure on Cuba, given the low transport and insurance costs associated with trading with the island, as well as Cuba's low trade barriers. These pressures, as is often the case, ultimately made Cuba's economy more efficient and competitive. This, in turn, helped Cuba achieve the levels of per capita income and overall standards of living that have been evidenced throughout this book and placed the country in very strong footing for continued economic expansion.

Condition III: Political, Social, and Institutional Conditions for Growth

Rostow's third condition for a country to be in a stage of take-off in its economic development—the realization by the nation's political and economic leaders that this was indeed an important goal, and that this feeling be shared by the country's population—was also amply evident in Cuba before 1959.

Cuba's Constitution of 1940, one of the most progressive of its time, made economic development and diversification primary goals for the country. It defined government as a promoter of development specifying that it should be focused on undertaking initiatives that would foment sustainable growth by private enterprise. It was in this context that, in the years just prior to the framing of this Constitution, and in those that followed, the Cuban government worked closely with groups from the international community and from the United States to identify the initiatives that could yield the best developmental results for the country. Among the most important of these efforts was a study conducted by the International Commission on Cuban Affairs in 1935, and another conducted by the Truslow Mission of the International Bank for Reconstruction and Development (the World Bank) in 1951. The earlier study recommended that the country focus on "[developing] non-sugar crops to take the place once held by sugar" and "sustenance farming to support the country population during the non-sugar dead season" while creating "an agricultural middle class."[18] The World Bank study highlighted the importance of further motivating the growth of the building, mining, tire, cement, and chemical industries. It also made important points about utilizing sugar as a springboard for industrial development by focusing on the industrial processing of its byproducts. This latter part is also one of the central points made by developmental economists Peter Bauer and Basil Yamey in *The Economics of Underdeveloped Countries*. In that book, they emphasize that, while differences in the natural resources of countries are not the driver of their development, the countries that have derived the greatest benefit from their natural resources are those that have leveraged that advantage by investing in their byproducts.[19]

It was also in this context, and under the guidance of the Constitution of 1940, that the Cuban government established the Banco Nacional de Cuba in 1948, and subsequently the Banco para el Fomento Agrícola e Industrial de Cuba (known by its acronym BANFAIC) in 1950. The latter acted as the Cuban development bank to support agricultural and industrial activities, as well as housing and small business. Later there was the founding of the National Finance Agency (Financiera Nacional) in 1953, whose purpose was to finance self-liquidating public works projects, as well as the Cuban Foreign Trade Bank in 1954, which was established to promote Cuban exports to countries with nonconvertible currencies (at that time most of the world). Finally, the creation of the Bank for Social and Economic Development (Banco para el Desarrollo Económico y Social or BANDES) in 1955, to extend short, medium, and long-term credits, as well as issue, buy, sell, and pledge bonds and other public securities, designed to stimulate low-income and general residential housing,[20] as well as to finance those through mortgage insurance (Fondo de Hipotecas Aseguradas or FHA), which previously existed within the BANFAIC. All these official institutions, together with the entrepreneurial spirit in the Cuban society at large, provided a strong backdrop for sustainable development.

Antonio Jorge, former professor emeritus of social sciences at Florida International University, aptly summarized the many important social conditions for sustainable growth that were very much present in Cuba at the end of the 1950s: "the island population modernizing attitudes toward economic activity and life . . . the people's familiarity and historical involvement with international trade . . . the degree of political participation and social awareness of a large majority of the country's inhabitants . . . the firmly entrenched tradition of small entrepreneurship and petty trading . . . the large middle sectors and their degrees of urbanization . . . the participation in the society at large, as well as in the civil service, of an extensive professional and technical population segment . . . the long and many sided relations between the United States and Cuba, and the pervasive influence of the former's ethos and lifestyles on the latter's ambiance and social atmosphere."[21]

These conditions all bode extremely well for the ongoing development of the island, which, atop the impressive accomplishments realized by the young Cuban republic discussed in this book, would have led to Cuba being a shining example of development in the region, and could have continued to place it today among the European peers with which it compared then. This would have afforded Cuba with developed-nation standing, instead of its current condition as a greatly deteriorated time capsule whose developmental metrics place it in the company of some of the most underdeveloped nations in the world.

Notes

1. Rostow, Walt W. *The Stages of Economic Growth: A Non-Communist Manifesto.* Cambridge: Cambridge University Press, 1961. 7, 36–39.
2. Rostow also treats this topic at length in: Rostow, Walt W. *The Process of Economic Growth.* New York: Norton, 1952.
3. Rostow, Walt W. *The Stages of Economic Growth: A Non-Communist Manifesto.* Cambridge: Cambridge University Press, 1961. 36–37.
4. Pazos, Felipe. *Medio Siglo de Política Económica Latino Americana.* Caracas: Academia Nacional de Ciencias Económicas, 1992. 1135.
5. United States Department of Commerce, op. cit., pg. 112.
6. Ibid., pg. 111.
7. Ibid., pg. 111.
8. Ibid., pg. 112.
9. Ibid., pg. 113.

10. Ibid., pg. 112.
11. Cuban Economic Research Project, University of Miami. *A Study on Cuba.* Coral Gables: University of Miami Press, 1965. Pg. 137.
12. United Nations, Food and Agriculture Organization (FAO). *Monthly Bulletin of Agricultural and Economic Statistics.* 7 (1958).
13. Mestre, Jose A. *The Cuba Castro-Communism Destroyed.* Coral Gables: University of Miami Press, 1961. Table 5.
14. Cuban Banking Study Group. *Cuba: Past, Present, and Future of Its Banking and Financial System.* Miami: Cuban Banking Study Group, 1995. Pg. 49.
15. Mestre, op. cit., Table 5.
16. Banco Nacional de Cuba. *Memoria 1954–55.* Havana: Banco Nacional de Cuba, 1954.
17. Freyre, op. cit., pg. 41.
18. Commission on Cuban Affairs. *Problems of the New Cuba.* New York: Foreign Policy Association, 1935. Pg. 492.
19. Bauer, Peter T, and Basil S. Yamey. *The Economics of Underdeveloped Countries.* Chicago: University of Chicago Press, 1957.
20. Cuban Banking Study Group. *Cuba: Past, Present, and Future of its Banking and Financial System.* Miami: Cuban Banking Study Group, 1995. pg. 36–42.
21. Jorge, Antonio. "Ideology, Planning, Efficiency, and Growth: Change Without Development." *Cuban Communism.* 6th ed. Ed. Irving Louis Horowitz. New Brunswick: Transaction Books, 1987. Pg. 306.

7

Cuban Communism:
The Road to Nowhere

As this book has demonstrated, Cuba's overall economic indicators placed it at the top of Latin America, ahead of many countries in Western Europe and every country in Asia. While, naturally, the Cuban population continued to seek further economic development and progress, it can be stated with confidence that Cuba's political instability at the end of decade of the 1950s was not driven by structural developmental issues or the country's standings with respect to the standards of living of its population. Instead, the social and political movement that brought about the Revolution of 1959 was driven by a strong desire among Cuban society to remove dictator Fulgensio Batista from power, who had installed himself as Cuba's President via a military coup in 1952 under the guise of trying to prevent a fraudulent election. The removal of Batista and the reinstatement of elections that could lead to ongoing democratic governance under the Constitution of 1940 were worthwhile objectives. That document, which was regarded as one of the most advanced in the world, provided the Cuban people with rights and protections equivalent to those of the most advanced nations in the world.

On the eve of the Revolution of 1959, however, Cuba was still very much in the process of becoming more politically self-reliant after centuries of Spanish rule that were then followed by decades of significant US influence over the island's politics. The governmental and nongovernmental institutions required to support the long term veracity of the 1940 Constitution were still in the process of gaining strength and independence. While, as the last section of the previous chapter demonstrates, Cuba had advanced quite significantly in the political and civic realm with respect to institutions that were geared toward supporting sustained economic growth, the island still needed to make a lot more progress improving the integrity, strength, and independence of its various branches of government. Particularly acute among these priorities was the need to create greater independence between Cuba's executive branch of government and its military, from where Batista had emerged and drew his power.

Another important element of Cuba's political maturation had to do with Cubans learning to shy away from the politics of personality cults and swift political changes. In favor of those tendencies Cubans had to learn to place their trust and full commitment behind institutional processes and evolutionary rather than revolutionary politics. This, unfortunately, did not happen. As the movement to overthrow Batista gained momentum toward the end of the 1950s, Fidel Castro, a student leader from a wealthy family that had trained as a lawyer, emerged from the various groups that were collaborating in that effort as the new grander-than-life figure that would capture the imagination of the Cuban people. Central to Castro's popularity was his explicit commitments to reinstating the Constitution of 1940 and holding elections within eighteen months after ousting Batista. Disastrously for the Cuban people, Castro never lived up to his promises. After taking advantage of political conditions in Cuba to secure his grip over the country, Castro moved quickly to gut the country's government and nongovernmental institutions. Under the guise of protecting national interests from foreign influence he also nationalized all foreign businesses. And, then, through force and intimidation, he nationalized Cuban owned businesses to eliminate any remaining vestiges of Cuban life that was not dependent on the government and, thus, eliminate any last threats to his ability to ensure his own lifelong permanence in power.

A key tactic for Castro's government was the creation of artificial conflicts to justify government intervention in all elements of the economy and society first and transition to complete control later. A second key tactic included the publicized firing squad executions of opponents that terrorized the island and the jailing or exiling of those that disagreed with Castro's redesign of the country. The implementation of such redesign, however, was almost always misguided and relied on the "expertise" of revolutionary leaders that lacked the most basic of competences in the field of developmental economics and market systems and that viewed such systems as a threat to their dominance over Cuban society.

One of the first and most important changes introduced by the Revolution was agrarian reform and especially the creation of INRA (Instituto Nacional de Reforma Agraria), which eventually evolved to become a state within the state. The stated objectives of the agrarian reform were to promote effective exploitation of Cuba's land and water resources to raise the standard of living of the rural population. What occurred in practice, however, was completely different.

1. The Rationing System

Only three months after its initial four-year plan (1962–1965) was inaugurated, the government was forced to interrupt it abruptly. On March 24, 1962, facing significant supply chain malfunctions and widespread shortages, the Castro government imposed the most stringent rationing that Cuba had ever known, even in the most abnormal of situations. Virtually all the figures on which the plan was based were incorrect, and the planned production and growth rates responded more to unfounded enthusiasm on the part of the leaders and Communist technicians than to a rational economic analysis based on facts. This distortion was labeled by Fidel Castro himself as "revolutionary subjectivity." The list of rationed goods included lard, vegetable oil, rice, chickpeas, green peas, lentils, beans and legumes of all types, rice, laundry soap, detergents, bath soap and toothpaste, beef, chicken, fish, eggs, milk, evaporated and condensed milk, plantains, butter, coffee, sugar, clothes, and shoes, among other items. The rationing system became progressively more stringent and wider in scope, with a rationing booklet with coupons being established in July 1963. By the end of that year, all consumer items were either rationed, intermittently supplied, or in acute scarcity. This too became the case with most medicines.

Things not provided by the rationing system could be found in the black market, but people had to pay very high prices. To have a broad idea about how much prices increased in a five-year period we can look at a table in *A Study on Cuba*.[1] The table lists prices for selected products in 1958 and 1963. The prices for 1963 correspond to the black market. Unfortunately, the table does not specify whether these prices correspond to a particular month or are annual averages. Regardless, a simple comparison between these two sets of prices shows an average increase of 297 percent over this five-year period.

2. Collectivization

The agricultural sectors first affected by the collectivization plans of the Communist regime were those that required large extensions of land for an efficient operation, usually in excess of 30 *caballerías*

(995 acres). This was the limit ultimately imposed by the Law of Agrarian Reform under a single ownership or occupancy under normal production conditions. Cattle ranches, sugar haciendas, and rice farms were the first to be confiscated under the collectivization plans. These were well-organized and highly efficient production units. Some well-inspired people wanted diversification, but what prevailed was mostly the desire to eliminate private production in the agricultural sector. Only a few months after the Law of Agrarian Reform was in effect, confiscation and collectivization had the unintended effect of disrupting cattle production in the best ranches in Cuba. Most of the land used by these ranches had been planted with imported grass at high costs to better feed the cattle. These lands were plowed to plant such food crops as rice, corn, or beans. Typically the land was not appropriate for these crops. The net effect was negative because the elimination of cattle was not compensated with an increase in food supply. Additionally, the destruction of pasture forced the reduction of the number of cattle. In an unprecedented display of economic inefficiency and waste, prize animals were taken to the slaughterhouses. This destructive process continued, without interruption, all through 1959. As a result, early in 1960, a meat shortage developed. This forced the government to introduce the first meat-rationing measures. However, neither these measures, nor the import of live cattle from the United States and Canada, averted the progressive liquidation of the Cuban cattle industry. Meat at low prices was traditional in Cuba. Per capita consumption of meat in 1958 was 112 pounds per year. The collectivization of the cattle industry created such disruption that not even a meager ration of 0.75 pounds of meat per week (39 pounds per year) could be met. This also applied to dairy products such as milk, butter, and cheese.

Rice cultivation underwent the same fate as the cattle industry. The confiscations of rice plantations began after 1959. No compensation was paid to the owners, as in the case of all other confiscations under the Law of Agrarian Reform. The productivity of many plantations fell by more than 50 percent compared with 1958. This was the result of mismanagement by inexperienced personnel appointed by INRA.

Production of other food crops usually cultivated on farms of an area smaller than the maximum of thirty caballerías prescribed by the law also suffered considerable disruption. The main reason that explains low yields in such crops was the lack of interest on the part of the farmers who were still occupying the land. On the other hand, the lack of organization and inefficient production of the People's Farms did not allow the government to depend on collectivized production. Farmers were consistently hampered by a lack of equipment, seeds and fertilizers of poor quality, and numerous government restrictions and regulations—all of which led to continuously lower levels of production.

Tobacco and coffee were two crops of great economic importance in Cuba. Tobacco cultivation demands a special type of soil and special agricultural techniques. Tobacco was cultivated only in certain regions of Cuba, usually in small plots of land, in small units, with the combined resources of the landowner and the sharecropper (*partidario*). The Law of Agrarian Reform did away with this highly efficient system. Cuban tobacco production suffered an important setback, and the international reputation of the product was affected as well. By mixing low-grade tobacco with high-level leaves, they upset the American consumer and lost significant market share even before the US embargo came into effect.

Although coffee farms were of small size and therefore should not have been the object of expropriation according to the Law of Agrarian Reform, many of them were. These properties became part of the People's Farms. A specialized labor force critical for coffee picking was replaced with "voluntary battalions" made of city dwellers who, due to their inexperience, severely damaged the coffee plantations.

All things considered, the status of agricultural and cattle production in Cuba shortly after the Revolution was clearly chaotic and was severely impacting quality of life on the island. Similar to what was also seen in the case of the Soviet Union, the destruction of Cuban agriculture showed the inefficiency of collectivism, and by contrast, the benefits of a market-based agriculture.

3. The Economic Effects of Collectivization

Agrarian reform measures that attacked private property, disrupted the traditional organization of Cuba's agriculture, and imposed new molds affecting ownership, distribution, and transportation converted the government into an all-controlling giant monopoly. The efficiency criteria that prevailed in a market-oriented economy were replaced by those of a political and ideological organization controlling economic activity.

Ultimately, revolutionary legislation became more and more stringent: expropriating all farmers owning land in excess of 5 caballerías (166 acres) and setting aside the promise of distributing land to the farmers. The legislation established Soviet-type *kolkhozes* (collective farms) under the name of "sugar cane cooperatives," and Soviet-type *sovkhozes* (state farms) under the title of People's Farms. Finally, imitating the Stalinist campaign of accelerated collectivization, the cooperatives were abolished and transformed into state farms. The following table compares production under the market economy and the new socialist regime. Except for cotton, which had not been an important crop in Cuba before the Revolution but which the revolutionary government decided to prioritize, all other crops, livestock and its derivatives saw very significant declines that were, on average, just over 44 percent.

The failure experienced in the sugar industry, as a consequence of both the internal collectivization measures and the foreign trade policy of the Communist regime, had tremendous repercussions on the economic life of the country. In January 1959 the total area planted with sugar cane was the biggest since 1955 as a result of the large plantings in 1957 made in response to the high prices of sugar prevailing that year. When Castro assumed power in Cuba in January 1959, the sugar industry he inherited was in a very healthy condition. At the time of the 1959 harvest, the government already had taken over seven sugar mills through INRA. Even though the number of units confiscated was small—7 out of 161—the disorganization of sugar production increased dramatically during the year.

Once the Law of Agrarian Reform was enacted, the local agents of INRA intervened in private activities, causing a disruption of production in many regions, particularly in large *colonias*, where sugar was planted and harvested. This policy of continuous harassment and the prospect of future confiscations eliminated any incentive for farmers to plant more cane throughout 1959. In this way the fundamental base of Cuba's export economy was considerably weakened, and it had to turn to support from the USSR for its economic life.

Castro's reaction to the suspension of the Cuban sugar quota imposed by the United States in the summer of 1960 came without delay.[2] On the same day that President Eisenhower signed Law 86–592, the Cuban Council of Ministers approved Law N° 851. This law authorized the president of the republic and the prime minister to order, jointly, through resolutions, the nationalization by "forceful" expropriation of all property belonging to United States citizens or United States enterprises, or to those enterprises in which United States citizens held an interest. This resolution also confiscated the Compañía Cubana de Electricidad (Cuban Electric Company) and the Cuban Telephone Company, and property belonging to American oil companies.

Table 42. Agriculture and Livestock Production in Cuba, 1957/58 and 1963/64.

Products	Unit	1957–1958	1963–1964	Percentage change
a) Agriculture				
Rice	kilograms	172,500,000	163,630,000	-5%
Corn	kilograms	246,879,000	150,000,000	-39%
Beans	kilograms	36,935,545	32,272,000	-13%
Sugar	tons	5,909,491	3,820,000	-35%
Salad tomatoes	kilograms	105,000,000	38,000,000	-64%
Cooking tomatoes	kilograms	8,750,000	6,000,000	-31%
Henequen	kilograms	10,000,000	9,220,000	-8%
Cotton	tons	336	15,000	4,364%
Peanut	kilograms	5,600,000	900,000	-84%
Garlic	kilograms	3,026,035	1,363,000	-55%
Onion	kilograms	1,290,000	1,136,000	-12%
Sweet potato	kilograms	161,289,131	82,725,000	-49%
Malanga	kilograms	191,206,000	47,270,000	-75%
Yucca	kilograms	186,350,000	82,720,000	-56%
Potatoes	kilograms	167,335,718	84,000,000	-50%
Bananas	thousand bunches	4,760,000	2,100,000	-56%
Plantains	thousand bunches	430,500	84,000	-81%
Coffee	kilograms	45,300,000	20,400,000	-55%
Tobacco	kilograms	41,654,298	29,158,009	-30%
Cocoa	kilograms	2,150,000	1,130,000	-47%
b) Livestock				
Beef	pounds	459,250,000	252,000,000	-45%
Pork	pounds	237,000,000	39,160,000	-84%
Poultry	pounds	79,000,000	50,220,000	-36%
Fish	pounds	70,000,000	60,000,000	-14%
Eggs	dozens	26,978,000	16,186,800	-40%
Milk	liters	959,946,000	583,000,000	-39%

Source: Cuban Economic Research Project, *A Study on Cuba*, Coral Gables, Florida, University of Miami Press, 1965, pg. 749.

The confiscation of these American companies was only a prelude to the total nationalization of the sugar industry. Law N° 890, of October 13, 1960, ordered the "forceful" expropriation of all sugar enterprises that had not yet been confiscated.

The total confiscation of the industrial sector of sugar production, including its direct and indirect sugar cane cultivation, as well as other property, was followed by an attack on the Asociación de Colonos de Cuba (Cane Growers Association of Cuba), the organization that had included all sugar cane growers since 1934. After several unsuccessful attempts to divide this organization, which was in strong opposition to collectivization, the government decided to liquidate it. By an INRA resolution of 1961, it was ordered that the Asociación Nacional de Colonos de Cuba should thereafter be called Asociación Nacional de Agricultores Pequeños (National Association of Small Farmers or ANAP). This resolution ordered the replacement of all executives and representatives legally elected by the 65,000 colonos with a group of government-appointed officials. However, in spite of this elimination of organized resistance to collectivization in the agricultural sector of the sugar industry, the wide distribution of land existing in Cuba prior to 1959 made it difficult for the government to collectivize sugar cane production. Even in 1962, after three years of agrarian reform and the confiscation of numerous farms smaller than the maximum size of thirty caballerías allowed under the law, cane produced by the private sector accounted for 61.6 percent of total cane production. The volume and percentage of cane harvested in 1961 by type of enterprise, per the estimates of the Ministry of Industry, were as follows:

Table 43. Production of Sugar Cane by Type of Enterprise, 1961.

	Estimated Production in Millions of Arrobas	Percentage
Cane Cooperatives	1,280	36.6%
People's Farms	62	1.8%
Total Government Sector	**1,342**	**38.4%**
ANAP Members[3]	1,246	35.6%
Cane producers with less than 5 cabs	908	26.0%
Total Private Sector	**2,154**	**61.6%**
Grand Total	**3,496**	**100.0%**

Note: One arroba equals 11.5 kilograms. Source: Estimate by the Ministry of Industry reproduced in: Cuban Economic Research Project, *A Study on Cuba*, op. cit., pg. 756.

Along with total government seizure of the industrial sector of the sugar production and the control of its agricultural sector, the government dissolved the Instituto Cubano de Estabilización del Azúcar (ICEA) and the Sugar Arbitration Commission. The functions of the ICEA were partly assumed by the Ministry of Foreign Commerce, and partly by the Ministry of Industry. The latter had already absorbed the administration of confiscated sugar mills through its subsidiary agency the Empresa Consolidada del Azúcar. Sugar cane production, however, continued under INRA control—directly, in the case of Cane Cooperatives, and indirectly, through ANAP, in the case of small cane growers.

One of the most salient features of the Cuban Communist regime with respect to agricultural production is the so-called "voluntary" work. This system began at the end of 1959 with the purpose of carrying out public works of minor importance such as street cleaning, grass cutting in vacant lots, and other public jobs in cities and on roads. In harmony with the trend toward labor collectivization, and under the influence of many publicly displayed "revolutionary" slogans, this so-called voluntary labor was extended to the cane fields during the 1960 harvest. There was a decrease in the supply of skilled workers for sugar harvesting due to a high degree of general absenteeism, absences due to military training in the militia, and lack of interest from cane field workers in working under this new system. This state of affairs induced the government to organize the so-called "battalions of voluntary workers" to help in cane cutting and handling operations. A substantial portion of the cane cut in the 1961 harvest in the sugar cooperatives was cut by this "voluntary" labor.

From the standpoint of indoctrination, the existence of a voluntary work system permitted the gathering of people, in places away from their homes, to whom it was an easy to task to preach the Communist doctrine once the manual chores of the day were completed.

As a consequence of the continuation of the Communist regime in Cuba, the Cuban sugar quota in the United States, which had been in suspension since July 1960, received a drastic cut in 1961, when no imports were to come from Cuba. This situation was made official when the Sugar Act was revised and extended in July 1962. Cuba thus lost its traditional position as the major supplier of sugar to the United States market. By 1961 Cuban sugar exports were concentrated in the Soviet Bloc countries and Communist China, while the position of Cuba as supplier of many Western countries had considerably weakened.

4. The Sugar Crops

The Communist regime that took power in 1959 found national inventories well stocked, and in the sugar sector it found sugar cane fields capable of producing a sugar crop of a greater output than those of 1957 and 1958. There was also an economic organization revolving around this industrial activity that was the result of accumulated efforts during a century. It included highly specialized personnel in the cultivation of sugar cane and in the industrial process of sugar.

Without giving adequate thought to the consequences that a drastic change in the structure of the sugar sector would produce, the economic theoreticians of the revolutionary government initiated an extraordinary campaign aimed at making sugar unpopular. This culminated in the massive confiscation of the sugar mills and sugar cane lands. In the words of Ernesto Guevara: "sugar cane is a source of slavery for the Cuban people." The economic emphasis of the government was focused on a gigantic but poorly devised and artificial industrial diversification process that was supposed to improve Cuba's economic growth and social welfare, but which had instead disastrous consequences.

The initial agrarian structure popularized the "sugar cane cooperative" to replace the sugar cane farmers. No real effort was made to distribute land as was announced, in order to liquidate all vestiges of latifundia. On the contrary, latifundism was accelerated through the kolkhozes (collective farms) and sovkhozes (state farms). The agrarian worker felt the impact of the change, which imposed labor conditions and wage levels that amounted to a complete abolishment of the conquests made by the labor movement before Castro. The unions became mere administrative appendices of the government.

The sugar crop of 1962 furthered placed into evidence the missteps of the Revolution, with production declining to 4,815,200 metric tons. It was clear that upcoming crops would continue to suffer as a result of the mounting industrial deficiencies, the cutting of immature sugar cane, the disruption of the planting cycle, lack of parts and accessories for trucks, locomotives, and tractors, and the absence of stimulus for the agricultural worker. In the industrial sector, nine sugar mills were dismantled. This had to be done in order to obtain parts with which to maintain other sugar mills in operation. This is a process of mechanical cannibalism that continues to this day.

The 1963 sugar crop dropped further, to 3,830,000 metric tons, but was compensated by an increase in the price of sugar that year.[4]

The high price of sugar served to sidetrack the accelerated industrialization project in favor of the sugar cane industry. This abrupt reversal of Cuba's economic orientations coincided with a new agreement signed with the Soviet Union, after Castro's trip to Moscow. Complementary bilateral agreements were signed with Eastern European countries of the Communist Bloc. The international division of labor in the Communist world was acknowledged, and Cuba's assigned role was that of primary producer of sugar.

During 1964, the Cuban government adopted the policy of not publishing any data on the production and export of sugar. Data corresponding to the 1964 crop were never published, but well-informed contemporary sources stated that it did not exceed 3,600,000 tons.

The failure in mechanizing the harvesting of cane in order to solve the scarcity of agricultural labor forced the government to establish the "voluntary brigades" and the "compulsory military service." Many crops were not cultivated or harvested within the normal agricultural cycles, and productivity and yield were seriously impaired since most of the nonsugar agricultural crops coincide in this cycle with sugar cane. The final result was that not only sugar production suffered, but tubers disappeared from the market, beef continued under a rigid rationing, and the consumer went without primary necessities.

At the end of 1964 the outlook for Cuba's sugar sector and overall economy was gloomy. Not only had sugar yields continually dropped and the infrastructure of sugar production systemically been damaged, but the uneconomic use of the "voluntary" labor to drive sugar production also resulted in decreased productivity in the sectors from which these laborers had been displaced.

5. Relations with the United States

The evident Communist tendency of the Cuban revolutionary government, its increasing economic attachment to the Soviet Bloc, and the continuous verbal attacks of its leaders on the government of the United States brought Cuban-American political relations to a high degree of tension in 1960. Commercial relations between the two countries had already began to deteriorate as early as 1959 as exchange controls had diverted import trade away from the United States market in many commodities. The trade agreement with the Soviet Union and the obligation of sugar deliveries contracted by Cuba under its provisions were the last straw in a long chain of events which ultimately induced the executive branch of the United States government to submit to Congress a bill authorizing the president of the United States to suspend Cuba's sugar quota if such a measure was, in his opinion, in the national interest of the United States.

On July 7, 1960, President Eisenhower signed Law 86–592 extending the Sugar Act until March 31, 1961[5] and amending some of its provisions. The president of the United States was authorized to determine "the quota for Cuba for the balance of the calendar year 1960 and for the three-month ending on March 31, 1961 to amounts to be in the national interest." The same day the president of the United States established, "in the national interest," restrictions on Cuba's sugar quota for the rest of 1960. The quota was, in fact, suspended. Imports into the United States in 1959 amounted to 3,218,723 short tons. As a result of the restrictions, imports in 1960 totaled only 2,419,655 short tons, or 24.8 percent less than the previous year. As a result of the measures, Cuba lost its principal trading partner, and its economy was left entirely dependent on the Soviet Union and its satellite countries. Cuban retaliation was immediate. The same day the Cuban Council of Ministers approved Law 851 authorizing the president and the prime minister to order, jointly, the nationalization by "forceful" expropriation of all the property belonging to US citizens or US enterprises or enterprises in which US citizens held interest. A month later, by a resolution approved by the president and the prime minister all sugar enterprises belonging to US citizens were confiscated. These firms represented 36.74 percent of sugar production in 1959 and were put under the administration of the Administración General de Ingenios of INRA. The confiscation also included Compañía Cubana de Electricidad, Cuban Telephone Company, and American oil companies. On October 13, 1960, Law 890 mandated the total nationalization of the sugar industry. The law ordered "forceful" expropriation of all sugar enterprises. One hundred and five sugar mills belonging to Cuban citizens were confiscated. With this step the government seizure of the industrial sector of the sugar industry was completed.

6. Foreign Trade

In October of 1960, President Eisenhower signed a partial embargo on exports to Cuba and in January of 1961, in one of his last actions as president, he severed diplomatic relations with Cuba. In March of 1961 the United States extended the Sugar Act again until June 30, 1962. The president continued to be able to modify the quota, but it was left untouched. In February of 1962, President Kennedy signed

Proclamation 3447 declaring an embargo upon all trade between the United States and Cuba. Cuba's foreign trade in 1959 showed a favorable balance with the United States but a negative one with other countries. The overall negative trade balance was $35 million.

At the beginning of 1960, it became evident that a change in the structure of Cuba's foreign trade was impending. By 1964 Cuba had reduced its imports from the Western world from $435 million to $165 million, and exports to the democratic countries had dropped from $474 million to $75 million

The economic situation of Cuba showed a strong tendency to worsen. The balance of trade with the countries of the Soviet Bloc became progressively unfavorable. It was estimated that by 1964 this negative balance was more than $900 million. However, this figure did not include the debt Cuba had incurred with the Soviet Bloc for technical aid and other concepts. Reliable estimates established that Cuba's debt with the Soviet Bloc was $2,335 million, and $165 million with Western countries.

The financial situation of Cuba deteriorated too. Cuba had to borrow frequently from the Soviet Union in order to cover open letters of credit and other essentials required by the sugar and nickel industries.

Table 44. Evolution of the Price of Sugar, Dec 1963 to Jan 1965.

Dec 1963	13.20
Jan 28 1964	10.84
Feb 25	9.20
March 31	7.90
April 28	8.20
May 26	6.00
June 30	5.26
July 28	4.40
August 25	4.20
September 22	3.65
October 27	3.65
November 24	3.20
December 15	2.75
January 19 1965	2.35

Source: *Lambor, Riggs and Co. Sugar-Market Report*, reproduced in *A Study on Cuba, op. cit.*, pg. 763.

More often than not those loans were not paid in time and had to be renegotiated.

Another factor conspiring against Cuba's economic situation was the persistent fall in the price of sugar in the world market. As can be seen in table 44, world market prices for sugar fell from 13.20 cents per pound during December of 1963 to 2.35 cents on January 19, 1965, representing an 82.2 percent decline. This resulted from weak economic conditions in the United States and Europe, combined with strong sugar production in the developing countries.

7. Social Security and Labor Conditions

Castro first obtained control of Cuba's unions in October 1959, imposing Communist labor leaders against the expressed will of the union membership. From there, his government began to take measures against the working class, forcing it to forsake many of the conquests of the past. The working class began to realize that the promised "paradise of the proletariat," rather than materializing, became further out of reach with each measure taken by Castro's Communist government.

The Cuban government became, for all practical purposes, the only employer. Each worker was given a labor card on which all the details of interest to the government were registered (employment history as well as ideological dispositions.)

In an all-out effort to increase production, the government increased the daily working hours, and rest periods were restricted. Voluntary work was established as an obligation. Paradoxically, and even though the regime proclaimed that unemployment had been eliminated, there is proof that a significant nucleus of population was unemployed. They simply dropped from the labor force, joining the underground or black market economy. In addition, absenteeism and shirking were other reactions of workers against the unfavorable conditions that were enforced, even though lack of fulfillment of the goals established subjected workers to the loss of salary and other benefits. Work effort in general was limited by the compensation received in real terms: the rationing coupons established in July 1963, after more than a year with a temporary system.

Over and above this strong control, the government maintained two institutions that were a constant threat to those workers who did not completely adhere to the labor policy of the state. One was the forced labor camps, called "centers of reeducation"; and the other was the compulsory military service (from age sixteen to twenty-five years, for a minimum of three years).

With respect to remuneration, the Cuban worker was worse off than under the previous system. The increase in the cost of living due to the high price of consumer goods and the astronomical prices prevailing in the black market drastically reduced real wages.

In the field of social security, after six years of a Communist government the balance was not favorable for the Cuban worker. Soon after the Castro government took power, work began on the unification of all separate social insurances. No separate fund was established for the purpose of financing social security. The whole administrative apparatus of social security was placed at the service of the political interests of the government, and only those workers who were true partisans were granted high benefits and other advantages.

8. Industrialism and the New Economic Structure

The revolutionary government announced in 1959 and with greater emphasis in 1960 and 1961 that the country would march at an accelerated pace toward higher levels of modern industrialization. To materialize this spectacular and accelerated industrialization, the government confiscated between 1959 and the early part of the 1960s 80 percent of the 38,384 industrial units operating in the country, particularly large and medium-sized firms, whether foreign or Cuban owned, leaving the confiscation of the balance, represented by small industries, for a future date. The government, now the largest industrialist in the country, began to exercise its monopolistic control through "consolidated enterprises" that did away with the name of the firms and labeled them with numbers.

The working class expected that the government was going to pursue four specific objectives: (i) the creations of cooperatives within each industrial plant under control of the workers' union; (ii) the organization of administration boards composed of workers to direct and administer the enterprises; (iii) progressive increases in salaries by prorating the benefits previously received by the owners of the plant; and (iv) progressive reductions in the work schedule, so that the worker could benefit from additional leisure time and enjoy better labor conditions and a higher standard of living.

In the years that ensued, the new governmentally controlled Cuban industry behaved in diametrical opposition to all that was promised to the Cuban population and to workers in particular.

The reality of the Cuban workers now consisted of "voluntary" work brigades, the payment of low wages and salaries in accordance with stakhanovite norms, the increase in daily working hours, the loss of leisure time, and, finally, forced labor through compulsory military service. Not even the youth was spared, with the creation of juvenile work brigades, and compulsory rural schools combining learning with forced labor.

During the second half of the 1960s, two very important policy decisions color the continued decay of the Cuban economy. The first occurs in 1968. After the principal agricultural, industrial, and commercial enterprises had already been overtaken by the government and accounting mechanisms had been eliminated, a new "Revolutionary Offensive" took over all remaining forms of private property. This was particularly addressed to the existing micro and mini enterprises, like barbershops, coffee stands, small stores, household repair activities, etc. It was the final knell for all private property, including places of abode (houses, apartments, etc.).

The other major change occurred the following two years. With the proceeds from sugar exports slumping, Fidel Castro again led the charge for a momentous policy change. With agricultural and cattle ranching in a continuous downfall, he "borrowed" the land devoted to those endeavors, for the planting of sugar. The objective: to produce ten million tons of sugar to enlarge the value of Cuban sugar exports. Of course, no consideration was given to the impact such a bumper crop would have on the price of the sweet. Additionally, the disruption that redeploying resources this way would have on the rest of the Cuban economy was also not considered in the brilliant revolutionary calculus. To make matters even worse, even after all of the disruption, the goal was not achieved, with reported production totaling only 8.2 million tons of raw sugar being harvested in 1970 (about the same of that was harvested in 1952 through efficient market means without sacrificing the rest of the economy).

With the economy now in total shambles, the Soviet Union had to widely expand its aid to the Cuban economy. It picked up the overproduction at heavily subsidized prices (forty cents a pound) and sold Cuba petroleum and other products at enormous discounts. It ramped up its aid and loans to Cuba (which were never paid) and requested other Iron Curtain countries to help in the rescue. In the early 1970s, Cuba would begin the process of aligning itself with this group, the Council of Mutual Economic Assistance (CMEA).

Notes

1. Cuban Economic Research Project, op. cit., pg. 744, Table 522.
2. Cuba provided close to 75 percent of the United States sugar imports at the American prices, top in the world. Estimates of this subsidy of close to one billion dollars a year at 1960 prices, and the effects on the Cuban economy of its cancellation can be found in Jorge Salazar-Carrillo, "The Past, Present and Future of Cuban Trade," in Antonio Jorge and Jorge Salazar-Carrillo, *The Future of the Cuban Economy*, Collegium of Cuban Economists, University of Miami, Coral Gables: 2004, pgs. 359–363.
3. Most ANAP land was confiscated by the government in the next stage of private property confiscation during the 1960s. ANAP represented much less than 10 percent of Cuban agricultural in the 1970s, and was controlled in the distribution of its commercial production by the obligation to sell to the government (Acopio system).
4. The price of sugar in December 1963 was thirteen cents per pound and the average for 1963 was eight cents per pound.
5. The original expiration day was December 31, 1960.

8

The Cuban Economy from 1972 to 2002

The Cuban economy from the period 1972 to 2002 went through four distinct periods, each of which is considered separately below. As we embark on that process, it is worth noting that, in presenting the evolution of the Cuban economy under Communism, we have relied, as much as possible, on sources external to Cuba on the basis that they are more accurate than those released by the Cuban government. Statistics prepared by independent third parties or collated from a variety of independently audited sources are generally considered to be more accurate than those of the Cuban government, as the Cuban government's statistics usually have the agenda of hiding the government's failures and promoting often fictitious successes. For example, when considering sugar exports from Cuba, we have used in general statistics compiled by the International Sugar Organization ("ISO"), as they serve to cross-check the Cuban government statistics against import statistics from the relevant countries as Cuba's revolutionary government has a track record of regularly concealing or adulterating production quantities.[1]

Additionally, the accounting system used by the Cuban government has changed over the 1972 to 2002 period in ways that sometimes make direct year-on-year comparisons difficult. Namely, Cuba used the materials product system utilized by the Soviet Bloc in the early years, and in the later years it switched to the national accounting system used in the West. Some statistics were not produced for a period of time, or were produced on a different basis to previous years. In addition, an economy where prices are set by fiat, and not by scarcity and value, does not represent markets accurately.

1. The Cuban Economy from 1972 to 1989

After years of operating under a command economic system, in 1972 Cuba took the incremental step of becoming a member of CMEA.

As such, prices were set by fiat by the government and the goals of the economy were set in conjunction with other Communist states, mainly the Soviet Union. International trade was strictly conducted within the CMEA, with Cuba's role being that of an exporter of sugar, and to a lesser degree nickel, and minimally tropical agriculture and fisheries. Trade was conducted in Russian rubles. Imports to the island were much larger than exports, which required large amounts of aid and loans, part of the former being hidden in the structure of export prices that were several times those prevailing in the world markets, while the import prices of energy-related products were much lower than the prevailing international prices as well. One of the objectives of such a price structure was to stabilize trade and to provide the planning exercises with the appropriate support so that they could concentrate on commanding production. However, these objectives were never achieved.

The intention of the CMEA was that countries were to specialize in certain commodities/goods that would then be exported to other CMEA countries. Given that Cuba's role was fundamentally to produce sugar for the rest of the CMEA, there was substantial investment and emphasis on increasing Cuban sugar production to the extent that at one point in was intended that Cuba should be producing up to fourteen million tons of sugar a year, a target that Cuba's private industry had never previously attempted to even come close to achieving and which, despite of all of the concentration of resources toward that singular effort under communism, the island ultimately never reached. The export of sugar, and import of other commodities produced by CMEA countries, was via a series of barter agreements. In Cuba's case, it exported the majority of its sugar to the USSR and received oil and loans (primarily) in return.

The barter arrangement with the USSR was enormously beneficial to Cuba. In 1991, Cuba was still receiving seven tons of oil for every ton of sugar exported to Russia. A barter agreement based solely on international market prices for sugar and oil at the time would have given an "exchange rate" of 2.1 tons of oil per ton of sugar. This had several effects. First, Cuba's energy imports were extremely high, peaking at 15.8 million tons of oil per year in 1989 (more than two hundred thousand barrels of oil per day). These were the highest amongst developing countries.[2] In addition, Cuba developed a highly mechanized agriculture, as it had large quantities of oil available and was able to import machinery such as tractors cheaply from the USSR. Finally, Cuba in fact received more oil from the USSR than it needed, so it was able to sell excess oil in the international markets, thus generating foreign currency at effectively minimal cost. The disappearance of these subsidies and benefits was to have a substantial effect on the Cuban economy following the fall of the CMEA.

2. The Cuban Economy from 1989 to 1993

The fall of the USSR and Eastern Bloc in 1989 had an enormous impact on the Cuban economy. There are many articles dealing with the economic impact and recovery of most of the ex–Eastern Bloc states,[3] and to some extent the same impacts were seen in the Cuban economy. One important difference, however, is that most if not all of the former Eastern Bloc states were at the same time in a transition from a Communist planned economy to a free-market economy (at least to some extent). Cuba, instead, attempted to maintain a centrally controlled command economy but without the immense benefits of CMEA. The impact on the Cuban economy was rapid and highly detrimental. As a result, Cuba entered into what, as we further discuss below, was called the "Special Period," during which the government asked the Cuban people to endure even greater levels of hardship and shortages than before.

Perhaps the most telling example of the impact on Cuba's economy during this period is what happened to its exports and imports. Cuba's exports diminished by 76 percent during the period 1989–1993, as shown in table 45 below:

Table 45. Cuban Exports, 1989–1993.

(mm of USD)	1989	1990	1991	1992	1993	Percentage Change
Sugar and related products	3,959	3,690	2,670	1,300	820	-79%
Fish	127	125	115	120	90	-29%
Fruit	139	150	100	50	50	-64%
Tobacco	85	90	100	95	75	-12%
Nickel	485	400	245	200	120	-75%
Medical products	58	130	50	50	20	-66%
Other	473	320	270	235	100	-79%
Total Exports	5,326	4,905	3,550	2,050	1,275	-76%

Source: Central Intelligence Agency, *Cuba: Handbook of Trade Statistics, 1996*, Langley, Virginia, USA, 1996.

Cuba's exports decreased from a value of US$5,326 million to US$1,275 million in only four years. This was due to the fact that up to and including 1989, with the exception (to some degree) of tobacco and fish products, the great majority of Cuban exports were to either the Soviet Union or other CMEA countries (79.8 percent). Cuba's primary market (exports to the Soviet Union alone in 1989 constituted 48.7 percent of Cuba's sugar exports),[4] which traded with Cuba on terms that were artificially skewed to subsidize the island, disappeared in a very short period of time. It should be reiterated that the former Soviet Union maintained its assistance to Cuba through aid, loans, and favorable terms of trade. However, it notified Cuba in September 1991 that this arrangement would cease. At the beginning of that year, and from then onward, the commercial exchange would have to be conducted in term of international prices. Sugar production decreased by approximately 50 percent during this period; the impact of this on the Cuban economy is clear given that the sugar industry represented approximately at least 30 percent of Cuba's GDP.[5]

The effect on the economy is clearly more devastating if the import side of the equation is considered, as shown in table 46. Particularly drastic were the declines in transport equipment and machinery, as well as raw materials and consumer goods.

Table 46. Cuban Imports, 1989–1993.

(mm of USD)	1989	1990	1991	1992	1993	Percentage Change
Food	1,011	840	720	450	490	-52%
Raw materials	307	240	140	40	35	-89%
Fuels	2,598	1,950	1,240	835	750	-71%
Chemical products	530	390	270	170	150	-72%
Semi-Finished products	838	700	425	195	180	-79%
Machinery	1,922	1,790	615	350	235	-88%
Transport equipment	609	590	170	125	80	-87%
Consumer goods	276	225	90	50	50	-82%
Other	33	20	20	20	20	-39%
Total Imports	8,124	6,745	3,690	2,235	1,990	-76%

Source: Central Intelligence Agency, Ibid.

For a small, economy that is not self-sufficient, the unavailability of raw materials, fuels, chemical products, and semi-finished goods depicted in table 46, opens a gap that is immediately reflected in economic activity, compensated only by the level of inventories available in Cuba. In less than six months stocks would be depleted and production would depend on their replenishment. The collapse in trade would thus be reflected in domestic (nontradable) goods first, and then in exports. Investment goods shortages (machinery and transport equipment) would end up mortgaging future production beginning three years down the road. Food and consumer goods scarcities would immediately increase the harshness of the Cuban rationing system.

These extreme statistics are supported by data coming, unusually, from state university sources inside Cuba, which demonstrate that for the period 1992–1993, agricultural production in Cuban sank to between 25 percent and 40 percent of 1989 levels.[6]

Based on the country's trading performance, one can surmise that overall the Cuban economy contracted by around two-thirds, although Cuban GDP data post the Revolution are highly unreliable during this period. This impact was particularly evident in the agricultural sector, where inventory levels were most depleted as a result of the country's reliance on an agribusiness model in which the state owned the means of production. The lack of fertilizers, pesticides, fungicides, fuel, and repair parts decimated traditional agriculture and eventually export crops (mainly sugar). Cuban GDP contracted *pari passu*. This led the Cuban government to undertake a series of reforms in an attempt to arrest the contraction of the economy.

3. The Cuban Economy from 1994 to 1998

Between 1994 and 1998, a period which was also known as the "zero option period," the Cuban government undertook substantial reforms to reverse the contraction of the economy that took place from 1989 to 1993. We continue to look at imports and exports as the key indicator of the performance of the economy during this period, using the most accurate statistics that are available.

As can be seen in table 47, above, Cuban exports recovered between 1994 and 1996, but then suffered a substantial relapse. This was mainly due to a downfall, both internally and externally, of sugar activity. Meanwhile, imports of goods increased by 55 percent over the period, as shown in table 48:

Table 47. Cuban Exports, 1994–1998.

(mm of USD)	1994	1995	1996	1997	1998	Percentage Change
Sugar and related products	785	855	1,095	920	715	-9%
Fish	110	115	125	125	120	9%
Fruit	80	45	55	60	50	-38%
Tobacco	85	95	100	140	165	94%
Nickel	190	345	450	445	325	71%
Medical products	110	45	55	50	25	-77%
Other	110	135	120	130	225	105%
Total exports	1,470	1,635	2,000	1,870	1,625	11%

Source: Central Intelligence Agency, *Cuba: Handbook of Trade Statistics, 2000*, Langley, Virginia, 2000.

Table 48. Cuban Imports, 1994–1998.

(mm of USD)	1994	1995	1996	1997	1998	Percentage Change
Food	430	560	645	625	630	47%
Raw materials	25	85	100	85	90	260%
Fuels	750	835	1,065	1,100	650	-13%
Chemical products	190	300	275	295	260	37%
Semi-Finished products	225	390	425	410	440	96%
Machinery	245	410	500	580	710	190%
Transport equipment	115	105	140	155	160	39%
Consumer goods	85	135	170	190	245	188%
Other	16	23	38	47	44	175%
Total Imports	2,081	2,843	3,358	3,487	3,229	55%

Source: Central Intelligence Agency, Ibid.

During the early part of this period the key variable in Cuban economic activity, sugar exports, experienced a substantial recovery. Sugar exports brought in an additional $310 million from 1994 to 1996 in hard currency, largely driven by an almost 50 percent increase in international prices. Nickel exports also expanded substantially (237 percent) over these same two years. Tourism grew rapidly during these years, beginning to challenge sugar's preeminence, although directly employing only less that 15 percent of the sugar workforce[7] and being even more heavily dependent on foreign imports. Toward the end of the 1994-to-1998 period, sugar prices began to falter, and nickel exports experienced an important retrenchment as well. As a result, total exports experienced only an eleven percent expansion over the quinquennium, with tourism having compensated for decreases in the other sectors of the economy.

Over this same period, imports experienced a net expansion of 55 percent, with only fuels declining as a result of Cuba expanding its domestic production. However, the value of imports contracted between 1996 and 1998, and when compared with 1989 levels only the "Other" category shows a small expansion, almost a decade later. "Consumer Goods" is the group that comes closest to the 1989 benchmark, but an important portion of these ended up serving the tourism industry instead of in domestic stores and, therefore, cannot be considered an expansionary force, except in net terms. The other important categories are still substantially below the 1989 levels and depict an economy that is certainly at less than 50 percent of the level of GDP attained in 1989. In addition to this dramatic decline, levels of investment in 1998 were between 25 and 30 percent below those of 1989, compromising the prospects for the country's potential future growth.

As a result of the weak state of the Cuban economy, the Castro government drastically cut budgetary expenditures across the military, internal security, and cultural and sports-related expenditures.[8] As a result, the fiscal deficit shrank dramatically, but still persisted (from 30.4 percent of GDP in 1993 to 7.0 percent in 1994 and 2.0 percent in 1997). Inflation declined, but these figures only represent the measured part, which produce artificial inflation rates, as rationing at fixed prices continued to be the norm for food, clothing, electricity, housing, sanitation, transportation, and many other requirements for day-to-day life. With the prospects of a westernization of Cuba, gross remittances and tourist expenditures from the United States began to exceed the $1 billion per year mark, and tourism from other countries also expanded.

If the export to import ratio in the two previous tables is analyzed, it shows a dangerously low ratio during these years, which keeps widening and requiring an increasing amount of the foreign trade gap to be financed from outside sources, notwithstanding the contributions made by tourists and remittances, which as we have seen previously in this chapter provide relatively little financing once expenses are taken into account.

As a consequence, Cuba's hard currency scarcity continued to plague the economy through the end of the 1990s. Total imports remained close to the level of 1991, the onset of the crisis, but now a substantial part of the imports were devoted to the needs of tourism, and of those receiving transfers from the United States, who used these transfers to purchase imports in the island's "dollar stores" (shops permitted by the government to transact in hard currency). The only way out, since Cuba owed large amounts to the governments that form the Paris Club, was to incur short-term debt with the trade suppliers and/or the government institutions that backed them.

As all kinds of Cuban creditors began to call and try to collect on their loans, in order to clear their books, Cuban became very hard pressed for dollars. The export turnstile began to quicken its pace, while on the other hand debt-for-equity swaps began to be implemented.

In the meantime, Cuba continued to use short-term loans to finance imports whenever possible. However, these were only available at increasingly high interest rates, due to growing market skepticism about doing business with Cuba. The result was that Cuba was often able to finance, at best, only the interest on such loans, and sometimes not even that, leading it to default.

During this period, the Cuban economy stabilized and then grew, as reflected in its foreign trade statistics; however, this growth was from the very low levels of 1993–1994, and a relapse occurred in 1998. The best estimates available for this period indicate that the economy reached, at most, about half of its pre-1989 crisis level by 1998. In addition, a large part of this growth was attained in a "foreign enclave economy,"—i.e., through dollar-based tourism and the country's dollar stores. At this time, the average Cuban worker still only brought home an average wage equivalent to US$10 per month and was still heavily dependent on government rations. In addition, the value of exports in 1998 was less than in 1995, but the cost of imports had almost doubled in this period, from US$1,990 million in 1993 to US$3,229 in 1998. As a result, Cuba was desperate for foreign currency to finance imports.

4. The Cuban Economy from 1999 to 2002

By 1999 Cuban exports had declined in value to $1,560 million (including molasses and honey), from $1,625 million the previous year. More than half of this was devoted to complying with their barter agreement with Russia. The second most important buyer was China, for a value of $56 million. Japan, Portugal, and Canada followed with somewhat less than half the previous figure each. The importance of the above is that Russia and China were barter deals, not bringing in hard currency. These patterns persisted in the next three years.

This period between 1999 and 2002 was a continuation of the reversals seen during the 1994 to 1998 period. As can be seen in table 49, sugar production fell by 9 percent over the period. Also, with the moderate economic liberalization that had been allowed by the government during the period from 1994 to 1996 being reversed, exports and imports began to contract again. As table 50 summarizes, Cuban exports fell to $1,268 million by 2002, corresponding to a decline of 19 percent over the three-year period.

Since its experimentation with dollarizing its economy and allowing for a modicum of private enterprise caused the Cuban government to worry that it could lose its tight grip over Cuban society, it quickly did an about-face and, under the orders of Fidel Castro, "rectified" to a more closed system—as it had done under similar circumstances in 1986. The small sole proprietorships that had been allowed to operate under very strict limitations (for example, hiring only family members) were burdened by confiscatory taxes and fees that caused them to close.

Table 49. Sugar Production, 1999–2002.

(mms of tons)	1999	2000	2001	2002	Percentage Change
Sugar Production	3.87	4.06	3.75	3.52	-9%

Source: International Sugar Organization, *Sugar Year Book*, London, various years. As reported by the Cuban government, but additionally checked.

Table 50. Cuban Exports, 1999–2002.

(mm of USD)	1999	2002	Percentage Change
Value of Goods Exported	1,560	1,268	-19%

Source: Central Intelligence Agency, op. cit., and International Monetary Fund, *Direction of Trade Statistics Yearbook*, Washington, DC, 2003.

Table 51. Cuban Imports, 1999–2002.

(mm of USD)	1999	2002	Percentage Change
Value of Goods Exported	3,355	2,153	-36%

Source: Central Intelligence Agency, op. cit., and International Monetary Fund, Ibid.

At the same time, the Banco Nacional de Cuba, which had underwritten the debt obligations of a large number of state enterprises, was left as an empty shell, full of these debts, but with no means of repayment, undermining any possible convertibility of the Cuban currency. Not only was a new Banco Central de Cuba created, but also close to fifteen new financial organisms were put in place. Concurrently, foreign investors were harassed and external creditors were held at bay, which about then began retreating from Cuba. As a result, domestic production suffered, and, lacking hard currency imports that could serve to invest in future growth and to cover current necessities, investment also suffered. As table 51 summarizes, Cuban imports dropped by 36 percent, from $3,355 million to $2,153 million, between 1999 and 2002.

Notes

1. G.B. Hagelberg and Jose Alvarez, "Cuba's Costs of Sugar Production: Past, Present and Future," in Jorge F. Perez-Lopez and Jose Alvarez, eds. *Reinventing the Cuban Sugar Agroindustry*, Lexington Books, 2005.
2. See Nicolas Rivero, "Cuban Trade Policy in a Transition," in *Cuba in Transition*, Volume 3, Association for the Study of the Cuban Economy, Washington, DC, 1993, pg. 295 and "Thoughts on the Cuban Sugar Industry," in *Cuba in Transition*, Volume 2, 1992, pg. 126.
3. Consult Jan Svejnar, "Transition Economies: Performance and Challenges," *Journal of Economic Perspectives*, Vol. 16, Number 1, 2002.
4. United Nations Economic Commission for Latin America and the Caribbean (ECLAC), *The Cuban Economy. Structural Reforms and Economic Performance in 1990s*, LC/MEX/R.746/Rev. 1, 6 December 2001.
5. Refer to Henry C. Wallich, *Monetary Problems of an Export Economy. The Cuban Experience 1914–1947*, Harvard University Press, 1960.
6. See chapter on the topic in Antonio Jorge and Jorge Salazar-Carrillo, eds., *The Economics of the Caribbean Basin: Present Problems and Future Trends*, University of Stockholm, 1997.
7. See United Nations Economic Commission for Latin America and the Caribbean, (ECLAC), *La Economia Cubana*, Fondo de Cultura Economica, Mexico D.F., 2000, pg. 515.
8. Review United Nations, Economic Commission for Latin America and the Caribbean (ECLAC), Ibid.

9

A Review of the Collapse of Cuba's Largest Industry

The first economic treatise on Cuba in the English language was written by the late Yale professor of economics and former Federal Reserve Board Member Henry C. Wallich. This seminal work was *Monetary Problems of an Export Economy: The Cuban Experience, 1914–1947*. In the preface he writes: "Cuba, with its almost exclusive reliance upon sugar exports, exhibits in an extreme form some of the problems peculiar to many export economies that have not achieved advanced economic development."[1] This dependence can be used to a country's advantage if the substantial expansion of the leading sector in an economy—through market mechanisms and as fomented by government agencies—leads to the growth and development of other sectors of the economy. By the end of the 1940s, Cuba had been able to piggyback on the expansion in the value of sugar production in such a way that Wallich's work acknowledges that "it seems safe to say that among all tropical countries Cuba has the highest per capita income. This income is produced by a highly capitalized economy concentrating upon a single export product, sugar. By pushing specialization to an unusual extent, the Cuban economy has been able to turn in an exceptional performance."[2] The same conclusion was arrived at by the Cuban Economic Research Group, which was gathered by the University of Miami late in 1960. "Together with the expansion in sugar production . . . growth took place in the other productive sectors."[3] The growth in these other productive sectors, which became even more important in the 1950s, led to the impressive levels of economic development that were captured in chapters 2 through 6 of this book. In stark contrast, during the period post the Revolution, the inefficiencies and systemic shortcomings of Cuba's command economic system meant that as the country expanded sugar production to sustain itself under far less efficient means of production, there were no positive corollary benefits to the Cuban economy and, instead, other industries collapsed.

As discussed in the first section of chapter 8, the intention under CMEA was that Cuba would provide the majority of the sugar required by CMEA member states, with a plan to increase production to fourteen million tons. The attempt to reach this level of production, which was ultimately never attained, relied on large subsidies of oil and mechanical equipment from the Soviet Union and a philosophical approach modeled after Soviet-style "gigantism," whereby increasingly large areas of land were dedicated to the production of sugar, utilizing large quantities of fertilizers and pesticides. Such a production methodology in effect takes no account of the input costs of production and focuses on simply increasing production via any means necessary, not increased production via greater efficiency. Consequently, Cuba became less and less efficient at sugar production, with the cost for each ton of sugar produced becoming progressively higher over time.

Notwithstanding the fact that accurate information regarding two key costs of centrifugal sugar production, agricultural and transport costs, are difficult to estimate in Cuba, statistics indicate that the cost of production of Cuban sugar became substantially higher than in other major sugar-producing nations during the Communist period. The information available for the production costs place them in the range of seven to eight cents a pound in the mid-1970s, rising to slightly more than nine cents, in an efficient mill, toward the end of the decade.[4] Jorge Perez-Lopez adjusted these estimates for inefficiencies, resulting "in an estimate of average costs of 10.4 cents a pound in 1984."[5]

Sugar cane cultivation, harvesting, cleaning, and transportation, and later milling, derivatives production, warehouses, transportation to ports, and shipping were totally controlled by the Sugar Ministry (MINAZ) and the Foreign Trade Ministry (MINCEX). The "Union de Empresas Operadoras de Azúcar y sus Derivados", which was a subsidiary of MINAZ, was the body that coordinated the structure of the sugar-producing industry. Cubazucar, the subsidiary of MINCEX, took over the sugar at the ports, when it was loaded onto vessels for shipping. Both of these entities had provincial offices, but the power resided with the central offices at Havana. The prices of all inputs and outputs involved in sugar production were set by the Ministry of the Economy and Planning, and the relationship between prices and subsidies by the Ministry of Finance and Prices.

By the 1996–1997 harvest, under this highly centralized structure and now without the benefits of CMEA subsidies after the fall of the Soviet Bloc, the cost of sugar production in Cuba was estimated, conservatively, to be of the order of 19.9 cents per pound.[6] For the next harvest (1997–1998) a new study undertaken by Alvarez and Peña Castellanos estimated the cost per pound of sugar to be in the range of 20.2 to 21.9 cents per pound.[7] There was a bevy of estimates produced with the harvests of 1999–2000 and 2000–2001 by the Cuban government. Unfortunately, these are not believable, as they certainly do not include all farm costs, and imports are accounted at the artificial exchange rate of one Cuban peso per dollar (these were in between 14.4 to 15.0 cent per pound of sugar). In a newspaper interview the head of the sugar workers union stated a figure of 16.3 per pound.[8]

A good example of the inefficiencies created under CMEA and resultantly high production costs for the sugar industry can be seen by examining the degree of mechanization that existed in the Cuban sugar industry. Compared to the use of tractors in the 1950s, when Cuba was one of the leading sugar producers in the world, "Cuba's stock of agricultural tractors grew by 32.4 percent during the decade of the 1970s and by an additional 12.4 percent in the 1980s; in 1989, Cuba had a ratio of 43 hectares of cultivable land per tractor, compared to the Latin American average of 130 hectares of cultivable land per tractor . . . nearly one-half of the stock of agricultural tractors in the country (37,990 units) was devoted to sugarcane cultivation and harvesting."[9] At the same time, the harvesting of sugar had become heavily mechanized. The percentage of sugarcane cut by chopper-harvester increased from 45 percent in 1979–1980 to 71 percent in 1989–90.[10] This high degree of mechanization, established by central command as opposed to market forces, led not to greater efficiencies but instead to high production costs, high maintenance costs (and capital to import spare parts was scarce in 1990s), and, once cheap oil from the Soviet Union was no longer available, high fuel costs.

During the period 1989 to 2002, the global sugar market changed substantially. As can be seen in table 52 below, global production increased by 17.8 percent, with Brazil starting to massively export sugar for the first time (see table 53 below) after a massive increase in production (more than doubling production in ten years). In the meantime, Cuba was the only major sugar-producing nation to record to decrease its production over this period. Cuban production decreased by 40 percent and its share of world sugar exports stood at only 8 percent.

Table 52. Sugar Production in Selected Countries and the World, 1991–1993 to 2000–2002.

(thousands of tons)	Average 1991–1993	Average 2000–2002	Absolute Change	Percentage Change
Brazil	9,825.3	20,122.5	10,297.2	105%
India	12,911.8	19,892.6	6,980.8	54%
EU-15	16,826.6	17,198.4	371.8	2%
USA	6,775.6	7,553.1	777.5	12%
Thailand	4,383.5	5,988.4	1,604.9	37%
Mexico	4,040.1	5,167.6	1,127.5	28%
Australia	4,015.5	4,932.9	917.4	23%
Cuba	**6,232.6**	**3,775.6**	**-2,457.0**	**-39%**
Pakistan	2,506.7	2,702.4	195.7	8%
World	113,904.0	134,198.5	20,294.5	18%

Source: Sergey Gudoshnikov, "World Sugar Supply and Demand until 2010 and Beyond," in Jorge F. Perez-Lopez and José Alvarez, pg. 101. Based on the International Sugar Organization (ISO) Year Books.

Table 53. World's Largest Sugar Exporters, 1991–1993 and 2000–2002.[11]

(thousands of tons)	1991–1993 (Mean)	World Share (%)	2000–2002 (Mean)	World Share (%)
Cuba	**6,674.7**	**22.9%**	**3,141.9**	**8.0%**
EU	5,065.6	17.4%	5,659.9	14.5%
Thailand	3,025.9	10.4%	3,768.7	9.6%
Australia	2,810.8	9.6%	3,969.7	10.2%
Brazil	1,842.1	6.3%	10,353.0	26.5%
Subtotal	19,419.1	66.5%	26,893.2	68.9%
Total World	29,194.3		39,058.4	

Source: Sergey Gudoshnikov, Ibid. pg. 101. Based on the International Sugar Organization (ISO) Year Books and author's calculations.

The adoption of the Soviet mentality of increasing production without regard to cost was also apparent in the extension of the duration of the sugar harvesting and milling over the late seventies, eighties, and nineties. The average number of harvest days increased to 145, and milling days to 110, compared to 99 and 85 in the 1950s.[12] It also worth noting that production in the 1950s was substantially higher than in the 1990s. Longer harvests generally result in lower industrial yields. "In the 1980s these averaged less than 11 percent sugar (base 96% sucrose), extracted per ton of sugarcane ground, compared to the 12.75 percent average of the 1950s. This was primarily due to the lower average sucrose content of cane ground over a more protracted period."[13] Also contributing to the lower industrial yield was the fact that greater mechanization of the industry lead to greater extraneous materials reaching the mills together with productive cane stalks

A study for crop year 1998–1999, which is the most up to date with publicly available data, concludes: "the average production cost for the largest cane sugar exporters (Australia, Brazil, Colombia, Cuba, Guatemala, South Africa, and Thailand) was estimated at 9.7 cents per pound. Since three of the top exporters (Australia, Brazil and Guatemala) are low-cost producers, it stands to reason that Cuban production costs where above the 9.73 cents per pound average".[14] In support of this inference, sugar industry analyst James Fry stated in 1997 with respect to problems faced by the Cuban sugar industry, "a huge capacity producing half of what it used to, running up their costs to well over US 20 cents per pound."[15]

Another disadvantage that became increasingly obvious as the 1990s moved on was the inability of the Cuban sugar industry to add value to its traditional centrifugal sugar production. The diversification into refined sugar and sweets with higher degrees of polarization, like white sugar, as well as organic sugar, has not panned out. Cuba is increasingly at a disadvantage in producing and marketing products with higher degrees of polarization, and thus higher prices, not to mention the competition coming from high fructose corn syrup. Even though Cuba had 17 sugar refineries, with a daily capacity of six to seven thousand tons, its participation in the export of refined products has remained relatively small.

The result of the loss of CMEA subsidies was that sugarcane production decreased from a mean of 7.0 million tons per annum during the 1980s to 3.8 million tons in 2001. Cuba could not finance its sugar industry when it was forced to purchase oil and spare parts in the international market at prevailing prices.[16] In the sugar sector, since

> the primary cause of collapsing production was not any absolute lack of markets . . . but shortages of key productive inputs that had hitherto been imported; fertilizers and other agricultural chemicals, fuels and assorted machinery and parts for both field and factory. The magnitude of such shortages did not simply match the fall in sugar earnings but actually exceeded it. This was because the national economic crises was so acute that a major part of shrinking sugar export earnings

was perforce diverted to finance other imports considered to be yet more vital, most notably oil and food. Moreover, since a number of international financiers or suppliers would accept the proceeds of sugar exports as collateral for loans or commodities, the pressure on the state to maximize such earnings was extreme. Indeed, during the most difficult years ... the search to maximize sugar production (and thereby exports) was so great that it forced the adoption of harvesting practices that might have increased sugar production in one season, but only at the cost of lower production and higher unit costs, in the next.[17]

The inefficiency of the Cuban sugar industry, combined with decreasing market prices, meant that Cuba was receiving less and less money from purchasers of its sugar. The graphs below show the decrease in Cuban sugar production in the 1990s, the market price of sugar in cents per pound and finally table 54 shows Cuban sugar production for the years 1989 to 2002, with the average market price per pound and value to Cuba of its sugar exports.

As can be seen, the decrease in Cuba's sugar production took place at the same time as a decrease in the market price for sugar, thus more profoundly reducing Cuba's sugar-derived income over the period. In fact, tourism overtook sugar as the main source of income for the Cuban economy over this period.

In addition to exporting the bulk of its sugar, Cuba also retained a percentage of its production for internal consumption. This sugar is held at certain warehouses for gradual release to the population,

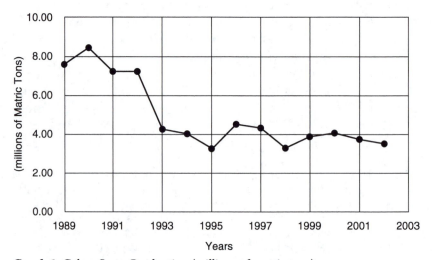

Graph 1. Cuban Sugar Production (millions of metric tons).

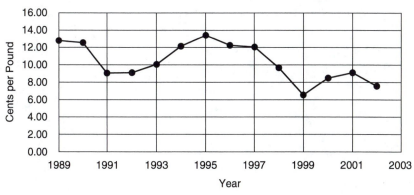

Graph 2. Market Price of Sugar (cents per pound).

Table 54. Cuban Production of Sugar, Its World Price, and the Value to Cuba of Exports.

	Production (mm of tons)	Price (USc / lb)	Value Exported (USD mm)
1989	7.58	12.79	3,959
1990	8.44	12.55	3,690
1991	7.23	9.04	2,670
1992	7.22	9.09	1,300
1993	4.25	10.03	820
1994	4.02	12.13	785
1995	3.26	13.41	855
1996	4.53	12.24	1,095
1997	4.32	12.05	920
1998	3.29	9.68	715
1999	3.87	6.54	560
2000	4.06	8.51	642
2001	3.75	9.12	589
2002	3.52	7.55	511

Source: International Sugar Organization, *Sugar Year Book*, several years; *CRB Commodities Year Book*, several years and *Wall Street Journal*, November 12, 2003; Central Intelligence Agency, op. cit., various years, and author's calculations.

tourists, and for industrial use. The quantity of sugar held at the end of the sugar production season is known as the "ending stocks," and the most accurate source of information as to Cuba's ending stocks is the International Sugar Organization (ISO). Table 55, below, shows ISO data on Cuba's ending stocks since 1989.

Table 55. Cuban Ending Sugar Stocks and Their Share of Total Production, 1989–2002.

	Ending Stocks (metric tons)	Ending Stocks (percent)
1989	301,199	4.0%
1990	637,093	7.5%
1991	147,457	2.0%
1992	339,129	4.7%
1993	127,143	3.0%
1994	291,979	7.3%
1995	366,946	11.3%
1996	395,412	8.7%
1997	398,293	9.2%
1998	408,543	12.4%
1999	376,788	9.7%
2000	305,557	7.5%
2001	422,372	11.3%
2002	274,659	7.8%

Source: International Sugar Organization, *Sugar Year Book*, various years. As reported by the Cuban government, but additionally checked, and author's calculations.

While Cuba's share of the world's sugar production decreased significantly, the island still badly needed whatever foreign currency the industry was able to generate in order to finance the many imports needed by the island. Therefore, Cuba was in no position to easily diversify into other areas of economic activity and away from sugar. Flawed production techniques and lack of capital only made this issue more acute. For example, increases in Brazilian sugar production were in large part driven by a desire to take advantage of increased demand for biofuels. Cuba, on the other hand, was not able to participate in biofuel production in any meaningful way. In addition, Cuba has not diversified into refined sugar and sweets with higher degrees of polarization, like white sugar. Organic sugar has not panned out as well. Cuba is increasingly at a disadvantage in producing and marketing products with higher degrees of polarization, and thus higher prices, not to mention the competition coming from high fructose corn syrup. Even though Cuba has seventeen sugar refineries, with a daily capacity of six to seven thousand tons, its participation in the export of refined products has remained relatively small.

Notes

1. Wallich, Henry C., *Monetary Problems of an Export Economy: The Cuban Experience, 1914–1947*, Harvard University Press, Cambridge, Massachusetts, 1960, pg. VII.

2. Wallich, Henry, ibid. pg. 3.

3. Cuban Economic Research Group, *A Study on Cuba*, University of Miami Press, Miami, Florida, 1965, pg. 1274. For a fuller treatment of this analysis applied to other primary products see Jorge Salazar-Carrillo, *Primary Type Export Activities as Leading Sectors in Economic Development*, University Microfilms, Ann Arbor, Michigan, 1967, and Jorge Salazar-Carrillo, *Oil in the Economic Development of Venezuela*, Praeger Publishers, New York, 1976.

4. As cited in G. B. Hagelberg and Jose Alvarez, "Cuba's Cost of Sugar Production: Past and Present," in Jorge F. Perez-Lopez and Jose Alvarez, eds., *Reinventing the Cuban Sugar Agroindustry*, op. cit. pg. 175.

5. Perez-Lopez, Jorge, *The Economics of Cuban Sugar*, University of Pittsburg Press, Pittsburgh, Pennsylvania, 1991, pgs. 116–117.

6. Hagelberg, G. B., "On the Trail of Cuba's Sugar Production Costs," in F. O. Licht, *International Sugar and Sweetener Report*, 130, 14 (29 April 1998), pgs. 221–224.

7. Alvarez, Jose and Lazaro Peña Castellanos, *Cuba's Sugar Industry*, University Press of Florida, Gainesville, Florida, 2001, pg. 87.

8. Cordero, Manuel, *Trabajadores*, July 8, 2002.

9. For this and related points refer to Jorge F. Perez-Lopez and Jose Alvarez, *Reinventing the Cuban Sugar Agroindustry*, op. cit., pg. 30.

10. Pollit, Brian, "The Technical Transformation of Cuba's Sugar Agroindustry," in Jorge F. Perez-Lopez and Jose Alvarez, eds., *Reinventing the Cuban Sugar Agroindustry*, op. cit., pgs. 51 and 52.

11. Gudoshnikov, Sergey, ibid. pg. 101. Based on the International Sugar Organization (ISO) Year Books and author's calculations.

12. Refer to Brian Pollitt, in Jorge Perez-Lopez and Jose Alvarez, op. cit.

13. See Brian Pollitt, ibid., pg. 53.

14. Refer to: Jorge F. Perez-Lopez, *Reinventing the Cuban Sugar Agro Industry*, op. cit., pg. 36.

15. Consult James Fry, "General named Minister of Sugar Industry," in *Economic Eye on Cuba*, October 20–26, www.cubatrade.org.

16. See Brian Pollitt, "Crises and Reform in Cuba's Sugar Economy," in Archibald Ritter, ed., *The Cuban Economy*, University of Pittsburgh Press, 2004.

17. Refer to Brian Pollitt, in Jorge Perez-Lopez and Jose Alvarez, op. cit., pgs. 56 and 57.

10

The Reconfiguration of Cuba's Economy in the New Millennium

The collapse of Cuba's sugar industry detailed in the previous chapter and Cuba's inability to drive sufficient domestic output to compensate for the combination of sugar's diminished contribution and the fall of the Soviet Union during the early 1990s meant that, as the twenty-first century began, Cuba was desperately looking for new international sponsors and new ways to generate income and hard currency.

Cuba's new sponsor arrived with the election of Hugo Chavez as President of Venezuela in 1999. Chavez, who identified himself as a Marxist and had previously attempted a coup d'état against President Carlos Andres Perez, quickly aligned with the government of Fidel Castro. The Castro government, which had been in the process of expanding its exportation of human capital via bilateral agreements with multiple countries, found in Chavez the perfect partner to expand its efforts. Chavez needed help remaking Venezuela's government struc-ture and establishing a number of social programs that could help him perpetuate himself as Venezuela's president. Castro agreed to help with both. Cuban know-how quickly began to be transferred to Venezuela in the form of governmental advisors and state police agents that could help Chavez undermine Venezuelan institutions and keep control over the opposition. In 2001, Cuba and Venezuela expanded their relation-ship and signed an agreement for Cuba to send 20,000 doctors and educators to Venezuela in exchange for 53,000 barrels of oil per day at preferential prices. This arrangement was subsequently expanded to 90,000 barrels of oil per day in exchange for 40,000 Cuban personnel.

The Cuban personnel sent to Venezuela, as well as other locations, had a duty to serve until the Cuban government determined that they could return home. Under this indentureship model, the Cuban

131

government also retains the lion's share of the proceeds it receives for the labor it exports and passes on only a nominal wage to the Cuban personnel. At the peak of oil prices, the value of the Venezuelan oil received by Cuba surpassed $3 billion,[1] which would make the leasing of human capital Cuba's most important export activity.

Similarly, starting in 2002, in the aftermath of Hurricane Michelle, Cuba acceded to allow for the importation of US food into Cuba, which has been allowed under provisions in the US embargo that carve out the exporting of food and medicine to the island. Since that point onward, while the Cuban government has continued to blame the US embargo for nearly all of its economic failures, the United States has consistently been the largest source of food imports for Cuba and one of Cuba's five most important overall trading partners. In 2013 for instance, Cuba imported approximately $359 million of goods from the United States.[2]

Over a similar time period, Cuba's reliance on tourism has also grown. By 2012, Cuba generated approximately $2.6 billion in gross revenues from approximately 2.8 million tourist arrivals.[3] This makes tourism the second largest contributor of hard currency to the island (see table 56). About half a million of the tourists that arrive in Cuba are Cuban-Americans from the United States going back to visit family and friends on the island, as permitted since 2009 under a relaxed set of travel regulations that were instituted by President Barack Obama during his first year in office. In addition to Cuban-Americans, visitors to Cuba also come from Canada—Cuba's largest source market, contributing approximately 1.1 million of Cuba's total visitors—as well as Europe, Brazil, Argentina, and China.[4] Despite of the recent growth, Cuban tourism still lags well behind other Caribbean markets such as Puerto Rico, the Bahamas, and the Dominican Republic. Furthermore, given that Cuba's hotel installations and overall infrastructure are generally inferior to what can be found in those markets, Cuba attracts lower-rated visitors with lower disposable incomes. As a result, Cuba only receives about $920 of gross revenue per visitor. Many foreign tourists choose to visit Cuba because they view the island as a "charming" time capsule (albeit a much deteriorated one). Such "charm" is of course largely lost on the Cubans that have to live with the endless inconveniences of being frozen in time. Also indicative of Cuba's currently precarious conditions is the fact that many other tourists are attracted to Cuba because of the extensive network of inexpensive prostitutes that they can find on the island.

These prostitutes are often underage girls or women who, though university graduates, have no better means to support themselves in Cuba's bankrupt economy.

Concurrently, while the Cuban government has never stopped maligning Cuban exiles, Cuba has no larger source of income and hard currency currently than the remittances that those exiles send to the island each year. These remittances first grew under President Bill Clinton, were then curtailed under President George W. Bush, and have since grown again after President Obama eased remittance and travel restrictions in 2009. Now, between cash and in-kind remittances made up primarily of clothing, medicine, and electronics, Cuba receives over $5 billion per year from Cuban exiles (see table 56). This figure represents a greater sum than the next four most important sources of hard currency for the island, combined. The significance of remittances to the island is even more pronounced when one takes into account the fact that remittances represent pure income for the Cuban economy, while other sources of hard currency have significant offsetting expenses (e.g. in the form of imported goods) that detract from the net income benefit to Cuba's economy.

In 2008, suffering from chronic illness, Fidel Castro handed over power to his brother Raul. In keeping with the standard operating procedures for the Castro dictatorship, this handover of power did not include an opportunity for the Cuban people to present alternate candidates or have a vote on the matter.

Since taking control of the country, economic necessity has led Raul Castro's government to experiment with ways to marginally open up the island's economy without sacrificing the Communist Party's totalitarian

Table 56. Sources of Hard Currency for Cuba in 2012.

Source	2012 mm of USD)
Remittances received in cash	$2,605.1
In-kind remittances	$2,500.0
Total remittances	$5,105.1 √
Tourism revenues	$2,613.3
Nickel exports	$1,413.0
Pharmaceutical exports	$500.0
Sugar exports	$391.3

Source: Morales, Emilio and Scarpaci, Joseph L. "Remittances Drive the Cuban Economy." The Havana Consulting Group. 11 June 2013. Web. 7 July 2014

control over the Cuban population. In general, the tension between these two goals has limited the success of any reforms.

In 2008 the Castro government removed or eased the restrictions that had for decades banned Cubans from accessing various goods and services. For instance, a decades-long, apartheid-like policy that banned Cubans from accessing the country's hotels—where foreign tourists were always welcomed with open arms—was lifted. At the same time, the government allowed Cubans to begin to purchase electronic goods, including cell phones. However, given that the average salary received by a Cuban is approximately 455 pesos per month (or about 19 US dollars)[5]—it is impossible for a Cuban, with his salary, to ever stay at a Cuban hotel, purchase a cell phone, or pay for expensive monthly cell phone service fees. The only Cubans that have the ability to do so, and a limited one at that, are those that receive remittances from abroad or high ranking government officials.

The second modicum of liberalization came in 2011, when the Castro government approved 181 carefully reviewed activities that it viewed as politically unthreatening for small, private enterprises to provide. The progress made by the small businesses that have emerged as a result of this new policy has been curtailed by heavy-handed regulation, high fees and taxes and the lack of a wholesale market. Furthermore, on several occasions, the government has entirely reversed itself out-lawing previously approved activities when it has felt that "too much" entrepreneurial success in a particular sector could lead to it losing its grip over the population.

More recently, in March of 2014, Raul Castro's government approved Law 118 to allow for investments in most sectors of the economy, with the exception of health care, education and the armed forces. The goal of the Cuban government is to attract at least an incremental $2.5 billion in foreign direct investment (FDI) to the island per year. It is doubtful, however, that Cuba will be successful at attracting sufficient FDI to have a material impact on the very low standards of living in the country given that the "arrangements" under which such investments can be made are generally unattractive relative to the opportunities available in other markets.

First, the Cuban government's lack of credibility with respect to the long-term protection of property rights and an arbitrary system for contract enforcement and dispute resolutions is a major deterrent for sophisticated investors. Second, Law 177 of the Cuban code continues to call for the Cuban government to serve as sole employer through which Cuban labor is to be contracted. This means that, in addition to having to agree to enable the Cuban government's unfair practice of retaining the large majority of the contracted price that it collects for each employee, investors also have to accept the fact that all hiring, firing, and wage decisions have to be negotiated with the Cuban government acting as a giant, omnipotent labor union. Lastly, while the legal framework stipulated by Law 177 allows for full foreign ownership of certain activities, in practice the Cuban government only allows for most investments to be made through either joint ventures, where a government owned company is the largest and controlling shareholder and where ownership transfer rights are often restricted, or through management agreements, whereby the ownership of the physical assets and means of production remains in the hands of the Cuban government.

Most recently, on December 17, 2014, US President Barrack Obama and Raul Castro announced that the United States and Cuba would commence the process of normalizing relations between the two countries. This change in policy, while certainly historic, cannot remove the majority of the investment and trade restrictions governed by the US trade embargo against Cuba, which can only be lifted through an act of the US Congress. Even more significantly, irrespective of US policy toward Cuba, Cuba's economic, political and legal structure will continue to significantly deter the interest of foreign capital and the ability that Cubans have to directly partner with such capital in order to improve their standards of living.

Notes

1. *Castrocare in Crisis*. Foreign Affairs. 1 Mar. 2015. Web. 1 Mar. 2015.
2. United States Census Bureau. "Trade in Goods with Cuba." US International Trade Data 2014. Web. July 2014
3. Caribbean Journal Staff. "Cuba Reports Record Number of Tourist Arrivals in 2012." *The Caribbean Journal*. 11 January 2013. Web. July 2014 and Morales, Emilio and Scarpaci, Joseph L., op. cit.
4. Caribbean Journal Staff, op. cit.
5. Oficina Nacional De Estadística E Información, República de Cuba. "Work Force and Salaries." *Anuario Estadístico de Cuba 2011*. Edición 2012.

11

Cuba's Developmental Standing after Fifty-Six Years of Communism

It is well know that Cuban statistics lack credibility as a result of repeated manipulation by the Cuban government. Nonetheless, Cuba's socioeconomic conditions have deteriorated to such an extent over the last fifty-six years that even the government's own inflated statistics tell a clear tale of economic destruction. Cuban statistics are so recognizably unreliable, that the United Nations Development Program's *Human Development Report*, the most reputable source for these statistics, demoted Cuba in its 2010 Report to form part of a group of small and weak countries with generally unavailable statistics. These countries are relegated to special tables at the end of the volume, and expunged from the main tables. Despite the statistical window dressing and recent attempts at reform, Cuba's stubborn adherence to a centrally controlled economic system means that Cuba's productivity remains one of the lowest in the world and, therefore, the Cuban economy is unable to provide for the well-being of its people. Cuba's own statistics acknowledge that the island's median salary is approximately $19 per month. Incredibly, this means that the median income of the island today is lower, even in nominal dollars, than it was before the Revolution fifty-six years ago. Such stagnation is nearly impossible to find anywhere else in the world. In the tables that we present in this chapter, it is clear that, while there are certainly more impoverished countries in the world than Cuba, that list has become shorter and shorter over time. Moreover, it is hard to find other examples where the actual magnitude of value destroyed can equal what has been seen in Cuba over the last fifty-six years. Even countries like North Korea or the poorest nations of Africa, although they have equally dismal or worse socioeconomic indicators today than Cuba, have not experienced

137

the same level of economic destruction that Cuba has experienced since none of those countries had achieved anywhere near the same developmental standing that Cuba had attained by the end of the 1950s.

In examining the tables that follow, one should note that, in some cases, the improvement that a country achieves with respect to a specific metric is most equitably measured based on the percent change that one country has been able to achieve, while in some other cases, the absolute improvement that a country achieves is a more equitable unit of measure. For example, if two countries were to improve the per capita GDP of their population by, say, $10,000 over a two-decade period, holding price levels constant, both countries would have provided for the same amount of incremental purchasing power for their people. However, if the first country had a starting GDP per capita of $15,000 and the second one of $2,000, most would agree that the second country, with a total GDP growth that would have been more than 7.5 times that of the first country and whose citizens would have obtained a much greater marginal utility from the incremental GDP per capita, would have economically outperformed the first. Thus from a comparative basis, looking at the growth rate in GDP per capita in that example does greater justice in terms of ranking the improvement experienced by the two nations than just looking at the absolute dollar improvement that was achieved. In the case of literacy, however, a strong case can be made that the growth rate in a country's literacy level is less relevant than the absolute improvement that a country achieves. For instance, if over the same hypothetical twenty-year period, one country improves its literacy rate from 40 percent to 50 percent, corresponding to 10 percent more of its population being able to read and representing a 25 percent gain in its literacy rate, it is hard to argue that such country has outperformed a second country that increased its literacy rate from 80 percent to 96 percent, which means that an incremental 16 percent of the country's population can now read, but whose gain represents only a 20 percent improvement over its higher starting base. Given this dynamic, for a number of the tables that follow, where it is helpful to do so, we rank each country first with regard to its standing in the world today and also provide each country's rankings with respect to its improvement both in absolute terms and in terms of percentage change.

Regardless of how one examines the tables, however, the clear conclusion that emerges for Cuba is that its world standing with respect to just about any developmental metric reported as of the end of the year 2014 is inferior today to where the country stood before the Revolution. The few exceptions that exist can be found with respect to certain educational and health care metrics where Cuba's rankings remain strong. Nonetheless, perhaps surprisingly for those who have been susceptible to Cuba's constant propaganda about how its achievements in education and health care have been miraculous, close inspection reveals that, given that Cuba's standing in these realms was already very strong prior to the Revolution, many other countries in the world have actually been able to achieve similar or greater levels of improvement in education and health care without having to resort to fifty-six years of totalitarian rule and destructive centralized economic control.

Reviewing Cuba's GDP per capita, table 57 reveals that the island went from being atop Latin America and in the same peer set or surpassing a number of European countries as well as surpassing every country in Asia, to now being surpassed by every country in Europe as well as a vast number of countries in Asia and Latin America. In fact, when one examines how Cuba ranks in terms of its percentage of improvement in GDP per capita, only two of the thirty-nine countries in our data set, Honduras and the Philippines, performed worse over the same time period.

Moreover, it is well known that Cuba's GDP data are among the most inflated of all of Cuba's reported figures. One of the ways in which this is evident is that Cuba's GDP per capita figure does not remotely tie to the wage levels in the country. Cuba reports that approximately 37 percent of its GDP is paid as wages (see table 59). If Cuba's GDP per capita were accurate, the multiplication of Cuba's GDP per capita ($6,106) and 37 percent would mean that Cuba's median income would roughly equal $2,259. However, Cuba's median wages are in the range of $15 to $20 per month and thus nowhere near this figure. In contrast, if one were to perform the same calculation for the United States, the implied median personal income that would be derived by the multiplication of the US GDP per capita figure of $47,882 in 2011 and the percentage of GDP paid as wages of 56.7 percent in 2012 (there is little difference in this metric from one year to the next), the result would be $27,149. This result is consistent with the fact that the United States Social Security Administration reported a median personal wage in 2011 of $26,965. In the case of Cuba, the inability to bridge between known wage levels and GDP per capita figures is likely driven by Cuba misreporting both

Table 57. GDP per Capita 2011.

#	Country	GDP Per Capita (in USD)	Absolute Change	Absolute Change Rank	% Change	% Change Rank
1	Luxembourg	115,377	114,307	1	10,683%	5
2	Norway	98,565	97,651	2	10,684%	4
3	Switzerland	85,794	84,570	3	6,909%	13
4	Australia	67,039	65,965	4	6,142%	14
5	Sweden	57,134	55,858	5	4,378%	20
6	Netherlands	50,215	49,518	6	7,104%	12
7	Austria	49,686	49,145	7	9,084%	7
8	Finland	48,887	48,236	9	7,410%	11
9	Ireland	48,836	48,391	8	10,874%	3
10	United States	47,882	45,741	12	2,136%	35
11	Belgium	47,807	46,890	10	5,113%	17
12	Japan	46,407	46,158	11	18,537%	1
13	Germany	43,865	43,123	13	5,812%	15
14	France	42,642	41,787	14	4,887%	18
15	United Kingdom	38,918	37,961	15	3,967%	24
16	New Zealand	36,874	35,704	17	3,052%	26
17	Italy	36,124	35,717	16	8,776%	9
18	Spain	31,820	31,505	18	10,002%	6
19	Greece	26,251	25,965	19	9,079%	8
20	Portugal	22,226	22,027	20	11,069%	2
21	Brazil	12,594	12,438	21	7,973%	10
22	Argentina	10,994	10,738	22	4,195%	22
23	Mexico	10,063	9,829	23	4,200%	21
24	Lebanon	9,165	8,853	24	2,838%	28
25	Costa Rica	8,676	8,402	25	3,066%	25
26	Panama	8,590	8,263	26	2,527%	29
27	South Africa	8,090	7,741	27	2,218%	32
28	Colombia	7,100	6,953	28	4,730%	19
29	**Cuba**	**6,106**	**5,727**	**29**	**1,511%**	**37**
30	Dominican Republic	5,512	5,273	30	2,206%	33

#	Country	GDP Per Capita (in USD)	Absolute Change	Absolute Change Rank	% Change	% Change Rank
31	Thailand	5,318	5,220	31	5,327%	16
32	Ecuador	4,526	4,376	32	2,917%	27
33	Paraguay	3,485	3,400	33	4,000%	23
34	Guatemala	3,178	3,018	34	1,886%	36
35	Philippines	2,370	2,176	35	1,122%	39
36	Honduras	2,250	2,084	36	1,255%	38
37	India	1,528	1,467	37	2,405%	30
38	Pakistan	1,182	1,130	38	2,173%	34
39	Myanmar	1,144	1,097	39	2,334%	31

United Nations Statistics Division; National Accounts Estimates of Main Aggregates; United Nations Statistics Division, 2011; Web; Dec. 2013.

its GDP per capita figures and the percentage of GDP that Cubans receive in the form of wages, since both figures are too shamefully low for the Cuban government to admit in its international reporting. Of the two metrics, however, the majority of the discrepancy is likely in Cuba's GDP per capita figure, as a result of the significant measurement distortions caused by Cuba's nonmarket pricing and exchange rate system. Therefore, while it is impossible to accurately determine Cuba's GDP per capita, the aforementioned analysis and the comparison of Cuba's overall economic indicators relative to other countries in the world make it likely that Cuba's GDP per capita is closer to a figure in the $2,000 range or below. This would place Cuba in the company of the least developed countries in Central American and thus some of the poorer countries of the world—a very different peer set from the one the island was part of before the Revolution.

Turning to trade, we have noted previously that competitive, modern economies tend to exhibit strong trading activity. While trade has expanded significantly over the last fifty-six years, with improvements in transportation and technology, Cuba's loss of global competitiveness has meant that over the last six decades Cuba has gone from being one of the most active traders in the world in the 1950s, with per capita trade levels similar to those of France and West Germany and higher than those of even the United States, to being one of the most closed and ineffective economies in the world. As can be seen in table 58, Cuba

Table 58. Trade Volumes in 2011.

#	Country	Imports (millions of USD)	Exports (millions of USD)	Value of Total Trade (millions of USD)	Total Trade per capita (in USD)	% Change	% Change Rank
1	Hong Kong	483,633	428,732	912,365	129,422	23,261%	2
2	Netherlands	507,759	569,513	1,077,272	64,836	9,829%	14
3	Switzerland	196,790	223,225	420,015	53,638	7,685%	21
4	Norway	90,787	160,305	251,092	51,335	8,456%	18
5	Ireland	67,167	127,012	194,179	43,464	14,104%	6
6	Austria	182,340	169,519	351,859	41,878	13,813%	9
7	Sweden	174,730	187,243	361,973	38,580	6,123%	28
8	Denmark	96,431	111,900	208,331	37,531	6,626%	26
9	Iceland	4,833	5,344	10,177	31,999	3,540%	42
10	Finland	84,235	79,126	163,361	30,434	7,585%	22
11	Canada	451,246	452,131	903,377	26,472	3,966%	39
12	Greenland	915	475	1,390	24,582	3,139%	44
13	Australia	243,700	271,697	515,397	23,004	5,608%	30
14	Hungary	100,989	110,897	211,886	21,158	17,680%	4
15	France	710,749	584,664	1,295,413	20,487	7,998%	20
16	Israel	75,830	67,648	143,478	19,336	6,388%	27
17	United Kingdom	638,940	478,460	1,117,400	18,003	4,493%	35

18	Italy	558,813	523,283	1,082,096	17,883	13,871%	8
19	New Zealand	37,346	37,484	74,830	17,131	2,279%	50
20	Spain	362,835	298,458	661,293	14,319	31,721%	1
21	Portugal	82,481	59,608	142,089	13,418	5,203%	33
22	Japan	854,098	822,564	1,676,662	13,165	16,565%	5
23	United States	2,265,890	1,480,290	3,746,180	11,997	5,990%	29
24	Poland	206,844	187,151	393,995	10,314	12,956%	11
25	Libya	10,506	46,016	56,522	9,357	11,311%	12
26	Greece	67,468	33,836	101,304	9,118	9,811%	15
27	Chile	73,545	80,027	153,572	8,954	7,007%	24
28	Bulgaria	32,579	28,222	60,801	8,228	8,844%	16
29	Thailand	228,845	226,412	455,257	6,856	18,430%	3
30	Romania	76,251	62,659	138,910	6,354	14,020%	7
31	Mexico	350,856	349,569	700,425	5,942	9,970%	13
32	Costa Rica	16,218	10,238	26,456	5,665	3,047%	46
33	Uruguay	10,623	7,997	18,620	5,522	3,816%	40
34	Turkey	240,842	134,907	375,749	5,209	13,256%	10
35	Venezuela	48,200	92,811	141,011	4,855	638%	61
36	Angola	20,228	65,745	85,973	4,398	8,044%	19
37	Jordan	18,463	7,964	26,427	4,094	4,302%	37

(Continued)

Table 58. (Continued)

#	Country	Imports (millions of USD)	Exports (millions of USD)	Value of Total Trade (millions of USD)	Total Trade per capita (in USD)	% Change	% Change Rank
38	Argentina	74,319	84,269	158,588	3,928	3,316%	43
39	South Africa	99,726	96,922	196,648	3,822	1,901%	53
40	Panama	11,342	785	12,127	3,297	2,272%	51
41	Paraguay	12,317	7,776	20,093	3,111	8,540%	17
42	Ecuador	24,286	22,345	46,631	3,109	5,451%	31
43	Peru	37,112	46,118	83,230	2,844	3,796%	41
44	Brazil	236,946	256,040	492,986	2,525	5,273%	32
45	El Salvador	10,118	4,979	15,097	2,428	2,148%	52
46	Colombia	54,675	56,507	111,182	2,394	3,092%	45
47	Albania	5,396	1,951	7,347	2,332	4,065%	38
48	Dominican Republic	14,522	3,728	18,250	1,822	1,669%	55
49	**Cuba**	**14,249**	**3,680**	**17,929**	**1,589**	**486%**	**62**
50	Indonesia	176,881	200,587	377,468	1,568	7,368%	23
51	Bolivia	7,551	8,107	15,658	1,542	2,983%	47
52	Guatemala	14,518	7,201	21,719	1,514	1,893%	54
53	Nicaragua	5,180	2,294	7,474	1,284	1,078%	59
54	Philippines	64,097	48,316	112,413	1,203	2,834%	48

55	Ghana	15,967	12,784	28,751	1,185	1,029%	60
56	Egypt	58,903	30,528	89,431	1,145	2,564%	49
57	Cambodia	9,300	6,950	16,250	1,131	4,613%	34
58	Nigeria	56,000	114,500	170,500	1,068	4,348%	36
59	India	464,507	302,892	767,399	637	6,972%	25
60	Mozambique	6,306	3,604	9,910	413	1,431%	57
61	Pakistan	43,955	25,383	69,338	400	1,235%	58
62	Haiti	3,018	767	3,785	382	1,638%	56

Source: Yearbook, Vol. II.; Total Trade; United Nations Statistics Division, 2008–2012; Web; Dec. 2013. Latest available trade data for Cuba is from 2008. The population figures utilized in order to arrive at per capita values are from United Nations, Department of Economic and Social Affairs, Population Division; World Population Prospects: The 2012 Revision; Total Population; United Nations Population Division, 2010; Web; Dec. 2013.

not only ranks toward the bottom of the world in terms of total trade per capita, but it is in fact the lowest of all sixty-two countries in the table in terms of increase in trade per capita over the last six decades of increasing global trade activity and interconnectivity.

Another salient feature of Cuba's economy of the last fifty-six years has been the increase that the country has seen in terms of economic power concentration in the hands of a small percentage of the population. By the end of the 1950s, while the sugar industry was still very important to the island, Cuba's economy was more diversified than it had ever been both in terms of the number of industries that had developed on the island and the broad distribution and fragmentation of ownership that existed within its various industries. That sort of economic structure yielded many benefits that ultimately translated into the attainment of the advanced socioeconomic indicators that were presented earlier in this book. One of those benefits was the competitive dynamics of the Cuban labor market, which translated into the citizens of the country taking one of the largest shares of GDP in the world in the form of wages. In contrast, given that Cuba's Communist government took over nearly all of the country's productive capacity within a short number of years post the Revolution, most Cubans today work for a highly powerful monopolistic employer. This monopolistic employer has, therefore, full discretion to unilaterally set wage and nonwage terms of employment. Table 59 shows that according to the Cuban government's figures, Cubans only receive 37 percent of the island's GDP in the form of wages. While, as previously noted, this figure is likely overstated, it still corresponds to a 42 percent decrease versus the share that Cubans were able to take before the Revolution. No other country in our data set has seen a larger reduction in this metric. Therefore, while commentators on Cuba's economy often point to the fact that there is less disparity among wage levels in Cuba today than there was prior to the Revolution (i.e. Cuba's Gini coefficient is low) that level of "equality" has in practice only been achieved by the Castro government forcing the country's entire workforce to accept extremely low wages. These wages translate into about one dollar per day even for most of the workforce—even including most professionals—place Cubans among the most poorly paid employees in the world. While the Cuban government subsidizes housing (generally in very poor conditions) and very limited rations of basic food and personal care items (of very poor quality) and provides free education (subject to great censorship and technological limitation) and health

Table 59. Percentage of GDP Paid as Compensation, 2010–2012.

Country	%	Year	% Change	% Change Rank
Japan	70.7	2011	45%	1
Switzerland	64.7	2012	5%	4
Denmark	64.2	2012	12%	2
Belgium	57.8	2010	6%	3
Germany	56.9	2010	-6%	5
United States	56.7	2012	-19%	10
Austria	55.6	2012	-7%	6
Canada	53.5	2012	-18%	9
Costa Rica	51.7	2010	-12%	8
Italy	47.7	2012	-8%	7
Chile	37.2	2011	-19%	11
Cuba	**37.0**	**2010**	**-42%**	**13**
Peru	23.6	2012	-41%	12

Source: International Labour Organization; ILOSTAT; World Comparison of the Percentage of GDP paid as Compensation to Employees; International Labour Organization, 2008; Web; Dec. 2013.

care (at greatly deteriorated facilities that lack basic medical supplies and medicines), the wage levels set by the Cuban government make it impossible for Cubans to operate as free economic agents to realistically purchase any goods or services that are not within the realm of the government's subsidies. This level of dependence on the government provides the Castro regime, by design, with an immense level of both economic power and broad control over the population. It also means that the very small group of families that control Cuba's monopolistic employer (the Cuban government) control the vast majority of the nations' income and thus are able to live extremely well relative to the rest of the population.

The low productivity of the Cuban economy means that today, regardless of subsidies, Cubans are able to consume a basket of goods and services that is inferior to what was possible before the Revolution, despite of the fact that fifty-six years of global economic development has taken place. The first metric that illustrates this is the number of automobiles that the country's population owns. As table 60 shows, the ratio of inhabitants to automobile in Cuba today is one of the highest, and therefore least advanced, in the world. Whereas in the 1950s

Cuba had fewer inhabitants per automobile than countries such as Italy, Spain, Greece, and Japan, today Cuba ranks as number forty-five among our fifty-nation data set, alongside countries like Honduras and Nicaragua. What is even more astounding is the fact that Cuba is in fact the only country in our data set and likely the world where the absolute number of inhabitants per automobile has actually *increased*. This means that while even the poorest countries in the world have become more motorized over the last six decades, Cuba has unbelievably regressed to bicycles, horse-drawn carriages, and hitchhiking.

Over this same period, public transportation has also deteriorated greatly. The rate of urban buses per capita before Castro, for example, was 1 per 300 inhabitants, whereas now there is one bus per 25,000 persons. These buses are themselves generally in terrible shape, emit vast amounts of pollutants, are highly infrequent, and are dangerously overcrowded with travelers standing claustrophobically jammed next to one another or literately hanging out of their doors. Similarly, railroad penetration, which was one of the highest in the world in the late 1950s, at 8.08 square kilometers per kilometer of railroad lines, had declined to 22.56 square kilometers per kilometer of railroad lines by 2010, with the trains that run on the remaining tracks also being in deplorable conditions.

Cuba's once impressive metrics with respect to telecommunications, media, and the press have also deteriorated drastically since the onset of Communism with all free voices having been silenced. Today, all of Cuba's newspapers and television stations are government owned.

With respect to television, Cuba went from having twenty-three television stations, representing the highest number of television stations per capita in the world and the fourth-highest level of television sets per capita, to now, in a world that has seen a tremendous proliferation of television networks, having only three television networks that are entirely owned and controlled by the Cuban government. Additionally, the decrease in purchasing power of the average Cuban has also meant that TV penetration on the island has actually gotten worse—a rare feat—as today there are forty-seven inhabitants for every television set on the island,[1] whereas before the Revolution this figure was twenty-two inhabitants per television set, representing one of the highest television penetration rates in the world at the time.

In the case of print media, all of the country's publications are also now government owned. Table 61 shows that Cuba has seen a 50 percent decline in the number of newspaper copies per one thousand

Table 60. Inhabitants per Passenger Vehicle in 2008.

#	Country	Inhabitants per Passenger Vehicle -Units	% Change	% Change Rank
1	Luxembourg	1.49	-87%	29
2	Iceland	1.51	-89%	24
3	New Zealand	1.62	-68%	43
4	Italy	1.69	-96%	11
5	Australia	1.81	-71%	41
6	Switzerland	1.92	-87%	30
7	Austria	1.95	-94%	16
8	Germany	1.99	-91%	21
9	France	2.02	-82%	39
10	Spain	2.06	-99%	4
11	Belgium	2.09	-85%	32
12	Sweden	2.16	-75%	40
13	United Kingdom	2.16	-82%	38
14	Finland	2.17	-94%	15
15	Norway	2.17	-91%	22
16	Netherlands	2.18	-93%	18
17	Japan	2.22	-99%	2
18	United States	2.22	-28%	49
19	Greece	2.24	-99%	3
20	Ireland	2.27	-89%	25
21	Poland	2.37	-99%	1
22	Canada	2.51	-49%	47
23	Denmark	2.65	-83%	36
24	Israel	3.85	-96%	8
25	Mexico	5.46	-94%	14
26	Uruguay	5.75	-87%	26
27	Brazil	5.99	-96%	12
28	Costa Rica	7.94	-90%	23
29	Singapore	8.40	-70%	42
30	Chile	8.70	-93%	17
31	Iran	8.85	-98%	6

(Continued)

Table 60. (Continued)

#	Country	Inhabitants per Passenger Vehicle -Units	% Change	% Change Rank
32	South Africa	9.26	-56%	46
33	Jordan	9.71	-97%	7
34	Panama	10.20	-84%	33
35	Turkey	10.87	-98%	5
36	Dominican Republic	11.90	-96%	10
37	Algeria	13.89	-84%	34
38	Colombia	20.00	-88%	27
39	El Salvador	21.30	-87%	28
40	Ecuador	25.00	-96%	9
41	Peru	25.00	-84%	35
42	Guatemala	28.72	-86%	31
43	Egypt, Arab Rep.	32.26	-91%	20
44	Honduras	34.48	-92%	19
45	**Cuba**	**47.62**	**+23%**	**50**
46	Ghana	55.56	-83%	37
47	Nicaragua	55.56	-68%	44
48	Kenya	83.33	-38%	48
49	India	90.91	-95%	13
50	Philippines	125.00	-65%	45

Source: International Road Federation; World Road Statistics and data files; World Comparison of Inhabitants per Passenger Vehicle; World Bank, 2008; Web; Dec. 2013.

inhabitants, as of the year 2004 which was the last year that this information was reported.

While it is the case that by 2004 significant circulation declines per one thousand inhabitants were witnessed across a broad cross-section of countries, the reasons this occurred in Cuba are very different from those that drove the declines in most other countries in the world. In most other cases, declines in circulation have been driven by increasing percentages of the population choosing to receive their news through the Internet. This of course is not the case in Cuba, where the rate of Internet penetration is one of the lowest in the world. As can be seen in table 62, Cuba currently reports an Internet penetration of

Table 61. Daily Newspaper Circulation per Thousand Inhabitants in 2004.

#	Country	Copies per 1000 Inhabitants - Units	Year	% Change	% Change Rank
1	Iceland	552	2004	42%	12
2	Japan	551	2004	39%	13
3	Norway	516	2004	38%	14
4	Sweden	481	2004	4%	17
5	Finland	431	2004	3%	18
6	Switzerland	420	2004	42%	11
7	Singapore	361	2004	72%	8
8	Denmark	353	2004	-6%	20
9	Austria	311	2004	67%	9
10	Netherlands	307	2004	16%	16
11	United Kingdom	290	2004	-49%	33
12	Germany	267	2004	-3%	19
13	Luxembourg	255	2004	-44%	29
14	United States of America	193	2004	-43%	28
15	New Zealand	182	2004	-53%	35
16	Ireland	182	2004	-25%	23
17	Canada	175	2004	-28%	24
18	Belgium	165	2004	-57%	36
19	France	163	2004	-34%	27
20	Australia	155	2004	-59%	37
21	Spain	144	2004	112%	7
22	Italy	137	2004	33%	15
23	Malaysia	109	2004	681%	4
24	Venezuela	93	2004	-9%	21
25	Philippines	79	2004	314%	6
26	China	74	2004	723%	2
27	India	71	2004	688%	3
28	Panama	65	2004	-47%	31
29	Costa Rica	65	2004	-30%	25

(Continued)

Table 61. (Continued)

#	Country	Copies per 1000 Inhabitants - Units	Year	% Change	% Change Rank
30	**Cuba**	65	2004	-50%	34
31	Lebanon	54	2004	-46%	30
32	Chile	51	2004	-32%	26
33	Pakistan	50	2004	459%	5
34	Dominican Republic	39	2004	45%	10
35	El Salvador	38	2004	-14%	22
36	Argentina	36	2004	-78%	40
37	South Africa	30	2004	-48%	32
38	Colombia	23	2004	-62%	38
39	Ethiopia	5	2004	830%	1
40	Angola	2	2004	-63%	39

UNESCO Institute for Statistics; UIS Data Centre; Daily newspapers: Total average circulation per 1,000 inhabitants; UNESCO, 2004; Web; Dec. 2013.

25.6 percent. This figure places Cuba toward the very bottom in the world, although the figure is, in and of itself, greatly inflated. The reality is that Internet penetration in Cuban homes is virtually nonexistent. Those that have access to the Internet generally do so only at their place of employment and that access is highly supervised and censored. A small number of government employees have rudimentary access at home and a very small subset of the population can, in rare occasions, use internet cafes relying on remittances from exiles.

In addition to Cubans being disconnected from the world and each other due to the lack of widely available and uncensored Internet access, table 63 shows that Cuba also ranks toward the bottom of world statistics with respect to telephone lines per capita.

While in many countries today low fixed-line telephone penetration is compensated by high mobile telephone penetration, this is not the case in Cuba, where there is only about one mobile phone for every ten inhabitants. Furthermore, those who do have cell phones can seldom use them, given that mobile telephone rates on the island are outside the reach of just about any Cuban who is not part of the government elite or who is supported by significant remittances from exiles. As can be seen

Table 62. Percentage of Population Using Internet in 2012.

Country	%	Country	%
Iceland	96.2%	Argentina	55.8%
Norway	95.0%	Bulgaria	55.1%
Sweden	94.0%	Uruguay	55.1%
Denmark	93.0%	Morocco	55.0%
Netherlands	93.0%	Albania	54.7%
Luxembourg	92.0%	Saudi Arabia	54.0%
Finland	91.0%	Kazakhstan	53.3%
New Zealand	89.5%	Russia	53.3%
United Kingdom	87.0%	Puerto Rico	51.4%
Canada	86.8%	Brazil	49.8%
Switzerland	85.2%	Colombia	49.0
United Arab Emirates	85.0%	Costa Rica	47.5%
South Korea	84.1%	Jamaica	46.5%
Germany	84.0%	Panama	45.2%
France	83.0%	Turkey	45.1%
Australia	82.3%	Dominican Rep.	45.0%
Belgium	82.0%	Egypt	44.1%
United States	81.0%	Venezuela	44.0%
Austria	81.0%	China	42.3%
Slovak Republic	80.0%	Tunisia	41.4%
Japan	79.1%	Mauritius	41.4%
Ireland	79.0%	South Africa	41.0%
Taiwan, Province of China	76.0%	Viet Nam	39.5%
Czech Republic	75.0%	Mexico	38.4%
Singapore	74.2%	Peru	38.2%
Israel	73.4%	Philippines	36.2%
Barbados	73.3%	Ecuador	35.1%
Hong Kong, China	72.8%	Bolivia	34.2%
Hungary	72.0%	Nigeria	32.9%
Spain	72.0%	Paraguay	27.1%
Bahamas	71.7%	Thailand	26.5%
Slovenia	70.0%	**Cuba**	**25.6%**

(Continued)

Table 62. (Continued)

Country	%	Country	%
Lithuania	68.0%	Iran	26.0%
Malaysia	65.8%	Ghana	17.1%
Poland	65.0%	Zimbabwe	17.1%
Macao, China	64.3%	India	12.6%
Portugal	64.0%	Pakistan	10.0%
Croatia	63.0%	Haiti	9.8%
Chile	61.4%	Iraq	7.1%
Cyprus	61.0%	Afghanistan	5.5%
Italy	58.0%	North Korea	0.0%
Greece	56.0%		

Source: International Telecommunication Union, Telecommunication Development Bureau, ICT Data and Statistics Division; World Telecommunication/ICT Indicators Database; Percentage of individuals using the Internet; Telecommunication Development Bureau, 2013; Web; Dec. 2013.

in table 64, Cuba ranks toward the very bottom of the world in terms of mobile telephone penetration—only North Korea, a close peer of Cuba's in terms of overall repression and economic backwardness, ranks below Cuba with respect to this metric among the countries in our data set.

The inability for Cubans to learn freely about what is happening in the world, together with the inability that Cuban's have to communicate with the rest of the world and, importantly, among themselves, have all been conditions purposefully imposed by the Castro government and the Communist Party in order to maintain absolute control over the country for more than fifty-six years.

Precisely because Cuba's standing is so poor on just about any measure of economic development and purchasing power, the Cuban government and its defenders have been vociferous about highlighting the country's stronger relative standings with respect to literacy and health. However, this chapter reveals that a long list of countries have actually outperformed Cuba in terms of advances in literacy and health care without having to resort to the dictatorship of a single family for over fifty-six years.

Given that Cuba's standing with respect to literacy and health care in the 1950s was already strong, the island's standing today in these two areas is, instead of miraculous, simply reflective of the rates of progress, whether measured in percentage terms or in absolute terms,

Table 63. Fixed Telephone Lines per 100 Inhabitants in 2012.

#	Country	Fixed telephone lines per 100 inhabitants	% Change	% Change Rank
1	France	61.9	645%	24
2	Germany	61.8	533%	26
3	Iceland	57.6	168%	37
4	Switzerland	56.7	99%	40
5	United Kingdom	52.6	265%	34
6	Canada	51.9	73%	41
7	Japan	50.8	974%	15
8	Greece	47.8	2231%	8
9	Australia	45.7	132%	38
10	Sweden	45.5	40%	45
11	United States	44.0	15%	47
12	Ireland	43.8	798%	20
13	Denmark	43.5	101%	39
14	Belgium	42.9	277%	33
15	Portugal	42.6	1051%	14
16	New Zealand	42.1	50%	43
17	Spain	41.1	725%	23
18	Austria	39.6	352%	31
19	Singapore	37.8	940%	16
20	Italy	35.5	479%	29
21	Hungary	29.8	1233%	12
22	Norway	29.5	55%	42
23	Venezuela	25.6	920%	19
24	Brazil	22.3	1410%	9
25	Puerto Rico	20.8	531%	27
26	Chile	18.8	726%	21
27	Turkey	18.6	2820%	5
28	Mexico	17.4	1178%	13
29	Finland	16.5	32%	46

(Continued)

Table 63. (Continued)

#	Country	Fixed telephone lines per 100 inhabitants	% Change	% Change Rank
30	Poland	16.0	931%	18
31	Ecuador	15.5	2415%	7
32	Colombia	13.2	623%	25
33	Guatemala	11.5	3386%	4
34	Peru	11.5	515%	28
35	Viet Nam	11.4	11549%	1
36	**Cuba**	**10.8**	**315%**	**32**
37	Egypt	10.2	1260%	11
38	Thailand	9.1	6050%	2
39	Algeria	8.8	454%	30
40	South Africa	7.9	44%	44
41	Paraguay	5.6	935%	17
42	Iraq	5.6	726%	22
43	Philippines	4.1	1385%	10
44	Pakistan	3.2	4398%	3
45	India	2.5	2707%	6
46	Ghana	1.1	189%	36
47	Nigeria	0.3	189%	35
48	Afghanistan	0.0	-92%	48

Source: International Telecommunication Union, Telecommunication Development Bureau, ICT Data and Statistics Division; World Telecommunication/ICT Indicators Database; Fixed-telephone subscriptions; Telecommunication Development Bureau, 2013; Web; Dec. 2013.

that have been matched or surpassed by many countries in the world. Moreover, as we discuss further below, when one goes beyond the headline figures that are often touted by the Cuban government, a number of important considerations make even clearer that, both with respect to education and health care, Cuba's performance leaves a tremendous amount to be desired. Commencing with Cuba's literacy rate, table 65 illustrates that the island ranks among the very top of the nations of the world. As such, Cuba's literacy ranking today is indeed higher than that it had in the 1950s. However, when one compares Cuba's literacy

Table 64. Mobile-cellular Telephone Subscriptions per 100 Inhabitants in 2012.

Country	Mobile-cellular telephone subscriptions per 100 inhabitants
Macao, China	284.3
Hong Kong, China	227.9
Panama	186.7
Russia	183.5
Finland	172.5
Austria	161.2
Italy	159.5
Seychelles	158.6
Estonia	154.5
Singapore	153.4
Lithuania	151.8
Botswana	150.1
Viet Nam	149.4
Luxembourg	145.5
Malaysia	140.9
Jordan	139.1
Chile	138.5
Guatemala	137.3
Switzerland	135.3
South Africa	134.8
Poland	132.7
Germany	131.3
United Kingdom	130.8
Costa Rica	128.3
Brazil	125.2
Czech Republic	122.8
Sweden	122.6
Thailand	120.3
Tunisia	120.0
Morocco	119.7
Belgium	119.4

(Continued)

Table 64. (Continued)

Country	Mobile-cellular telephone subscriptions per 100 inhabitants
Denmark	118.0
Greece	116.9
Hungary	116.4
Norway	115.5
Egypt	115.3
Portugal	115.1
Mauritius	113.1
Slovak Republic	111.2
Ecuador	110.7
South Korea	110.4
New Zealand	110.3
Slovenia	110.1
Japan	109.4
Georgia	109.2
Albania	108.4
Spain	108.3
Ireland	107.1
Philippines	106.8
Australia	106.2
Iceland	105.4
Algeria	103.3
Colombia	103.2
Namibia	103.0
Venezuela	102.1
Paraguay	101.7
Congo	101.2
Ghana	100.3
Peru	98.8
Cyprus	98.4
United States	98.2
France	98.1
Zimbabwe	96.9

Country	Mobile-cellular telephone subscriptions per 100 inhabitants
Jamaica	96.5
Turkey	90.8
Dominican Rep.	88.8
Mexico	86.8
Puerto Rico	81.7
China	81.3
Iraq	79.4
Iran	76.9
Canada	75.7
India	68.7
Nigeria	67.7
Pakistan	66.8
Afghanistan	53.9
Democratic Republic of Congo	28.0
Cuba	**14.9**
North Korea	6.9

Source: International Telecommunication Union, Telecommunication Development Bureau, ICT Data and Statistics Division; World Telecommunication/ICT Indicators Database; Mobile-cellular subscriptions; Telecommunication Development Bureau, 2013; Web; Dec. 2013.

gains against the same set of counties that were included in chapter 5, one sees that Cuba's gains actually place it in the twenty-sixth place in terms of both the incremental percentage of the population that attained literacy (i.e., the absolute change) or the rate of improvement that this literacy gain represented off of the country's starting base. As such, while Cuba's literacy rate is indeed high today and represents one of the few elements of Cuba's society that the Castro government has not destroyed, Cuba's improvement over more than five decades does constitute a particularly miraculous accomplishment. In fact, of the forty-two countries included in our data set more than half outperformed Cuba both in terms of the incremental percentage of the population that learned how to read and in terms of the rate of improvement in literacy levels.

Furthermore, a close examination of the overall state of Cuban education reveals that, while Cubans certainly are very literate, the

Table 65. Literacy Rates, 2002–2011.

#	Country	Literacy Rate	Year	Absolute Change	Absolute Change Rank	% Change	% Change Rank
1	**Cuba**	**99.8%**	**2011**	**22%**	**26**	**28%**	**26**
2	Poland	99.7%	2011	6%	36	6%	36
3	Italy	99.0%	2011	13%	33	15%	33
4	Hungary	99.0%	2011	4%	37	4%	37
5	France	99.0%	2003	3%	39	3%	39
6	Belgium	99.0%	2003	2%	40	2%	40
7	United States	99.0%	2003	2%	41	2%	41
8	Japan	99.0%	2002	1%	42	1%	42
9	Chile	98.6%	2009	18%	28	23%	29
10	Bulgaria	98.4%	2011	13%	32	15%	32
11	South Korea	97.9%	2002	21%	27	28%	27
12	Argentina	97.9%	2011	12%	34	13%	34
13	Spain	97.7%	2010	15%	31	19%	31
14	Romania	97.7%	2011	9%	35	10%	35
15	Greece	97.3%	2011	23%	24	31%	24
16	Israel	97.1%	2004	3%	38	4%	38
17	Albania	96.8%	2011	25%	22	35%	22
18	Costa Rica	96.3%	2011	17%	30	21%	30
19	Venezuela	95.5%	2009	43%	10	83%	14
20	Portugal	95.4%	2011	40%	15	71%	16
21	Philippines	95.4%	2008	35%	19	59%	19
22	China	95.1%	2010	45%	7	90%	12
23	Turkey	94.1%	2011	62%	2	195%	5
24	Panama	94.1%	2010	24%	23	35%	23
25	Paraguay	93.9%	2010	28%	21	43%	21
26	Colombia	93.6%	2011	31%	20	50%	20
27	Thailand	93.5%	2005	42%	11	80%	15
28	Mexico	93.5%	2011	37%	17	65%	17
29	Hong Kong	93.5%	2002	22%	25	31%	25
30	South Africa	93.0%	2011	66%	1	238%	3
31	Ecuador	91.6%	2011	36%	18	65%	18

#	Country	Literacy Rate	Year	Absolute Change	Absolute Change Rank	% Change	% Change Rank
32	Bolivia	91.2%	2009	59%	3	184%	6
33	Brazil	90.4%	2010	41%	13	83%	13
34	Puerto Rico	90.3%	2011	17%	29	23%	28
35	Dominican Republic	90.1%	2011	47%	6	110%	9
36	Honduras	85.1%	2011	50%	5	142%	7
37	El Salvador	84.5%	2010	44%	8	109%	10
38	Nicaragua	78.0%	2005	40%	14	103%	11
39	Guatemala	75.9%	2011	42%	12	121%	8
40	Morocco	67.1%	2011	53%	4	386%	1
41	India	62.8%	2006	44%	9	225%	4
42	Haiti	48.7%	2006	38%	16	364%	2

Source: Central Intelligence Agency; The World Factbook; Literacy; Central Intelligence Agency, 2013; Web; Dec. 2013.

government tightly controls *what* they can read. A large proportion of the world's fiction and nonfiction texts, for example, are viewed as subversive by the Cuban government and thus banned from the population. Similarly, as was previously discussed, Internet access among the general population is virtually nonexistent and what access is available is highly censored. And, there are no independent media outlets on the island. The combination of these factors means that Cuba's high literacy rate actually belies a highly misinformed population that is completely ignorant of very important portions of modern human knowledge.

Similarly, while Cuba spends 12.9 percent of its GDP on education (one of the highest rates in the world)[2] the precarious conditions of Cuba's GDP means that this still translates into educational facilities that are largely deteriorated and are lacking basic supplies, not to mention any sort of advanced technologies. Last, given the nature of the Cuban government, classrooms in Cuba are consistently used as vehicles for Communist indoctrination and intimidation. In addition to being inculcated with incorrect information to aggrandize the Communist party and the figure of Fidel and Raul Castro, Cuban students can also expect to be closely watched for any signs of thoughts or behaviors that diverge from those desired by the Communist Party.

Table 66. Life Expectancy at Birth in Years 2005–2010.

#	Country	Life Expectancy	Absolute Change	Absolute Change Rank	% Change	% Change Rank
1	Japan	82.7	16.4	27	25%	35
2	China, Hong Kong SAR	82.4	16.4	26	25%	34
3	Switzerland	81.8	11.1	45	16%	50
4	Australia	81.7	11.2	44	16%	48
5	Italy	81.5	13.1	36	19%	39
6	Singapore	81.2	17.2	23	27%	30
7	Spain	81.2	13.7	35	20%	36
8	Sweden	81.1	8.3	59	11%	60
9	France	80.9	11.7	42	17%	46
10	Norway	80.6	7.1	63	10%	64
11	Canada	80.5	10.3	51	15%	54
12	New Zealand	80.2	9.6	53	14%	57
13	Netherlands	80.2	7.3	62	10%	63
14	Austria	80.1	12.2	40	18%	43
15	South Korea	80	28.8	4	56%	10
16	Greece	79.8	12.6	37	19%	41
17	Germany	79.8	10.9	46	16%	49
18	Ireland	79.6	10.6	49	15%	51
19	United Kingdom	79.6	9.1	56	13%	58
20	Luxembourg	79.5	12.0	41	18%	44
21	Finland	79.5	11.5	43	17%	45
22	Belgium	79.5	10.1	52	15%	56
23	Cyprus	79	10.3	50	15%	53
24	Costa Rica	78.8	18.7	19	31%	23
25	Portugal	78.7	16.9	25	27%	29
26	Chile	78.6	22.4	14	40%	16
27	Denmark	78.6	6.5	65	9%	65
28	**Cuba**	**78.3**	**16.0**	**29**	**26%**	**32**
29	Lebanon	78.2	15.8	30	25%	33

#	Country	Life Expectancy	Absolute Change	Absolute Change Rank	% Change	% Change Rank
30	United States of America	78.1	8.5	58	12%	59
31	Czech Republic	76.8	7.4	61	11%	61
32	Panama	76.4	16.9	24	28%	27
33	Mexico	76.3	21.0	17	38%	18
34	Croatia	76.1	12.5	38	20%	37
35	Poland	75.5	9.6	55	15%	55
36	Argentina	75.3	10.8	47	17%	47
37	Viet Nam	75.1	17.8	21	31%	24
38	Ecuador	75	23.6	11	46%	13
39	China	74.4	29.4	2	65%	4
40	Malaysia	74	16.1	28	28%	28
41	Venezuela	73.7	15.6	31	27%	31
42	Turkey	73.4	29.7	1	68%	2
43	Peru	73.1	26.8	7	58%	8
44	Bulgaria	73	6.7	64	10%	62
45	Colombia	72.9	17.7	22	32%	22
46	Brazil	72.4	18.9	18	35%	20
47	Iran	72.3	28.8	3	66%	3
48	Dominican Republic	72.2	22.3	15	45%	14
49	Jamaica	72.2	9.6	54	15%	52
50	El Salvador	71.3	22.0	16	45%	15
51	Egypt	69.9	23.5	12	51%	12
52	Indonesia	69.6	26.9	6	63%	7
53	Cambodia	69.5	28.5	5	70%	1
54	North Korea	68.4	18.5	20	37%	19
55	Philippines	67.8	10.7	48	19%	42
56	Russian Federation	67.2	2.4	67	4%	67

(Continued)

Table 66. (Continued)

#	Country	Life Expectancy	Absolute Change	Absolute Change Rank	% Change	% Change Rank
57	Bolivia	65.6	23.7	10	57%	9
58	India	64.9	25.3	8	64%	6
59	Myanmar	64.2	23.0	13	56%	11
60	Papua New Guinea	61.5	24.3	9	65%	5
61	Sudan	60.9	13.8	34	29%	26
62	Ghana	60	15.3	32	34%	21
63	Congo	55.7	8.9	57	19%	40
64	Cameroon	52.7	12.2	39	30%	25
65	South Africa	52.2	4.2	66	9%	66
66	Nigeria	50.2	14.2	33	39%	17
67	Congo	48.3	7.8	60	19%	38
68	Botswana	46.5	-3.2	68	-6.4%	68

Source: United Nations, Department of Economic and Social Affairs, Population Division; World Population Prospects: The 2012 Revision; Life Expectancy at Birth; United Nations Population Division, 2012; Web; Dec. 2013.

Anyone that evidences such divergence can expect to be punished with expulsion and with the prospect of never being allowed to attend any of the government owned universities on the island (which are the only ones available), irrespective of the strength of one's academic record.

A similar review of Cuba's health care statistics reveals that Cuba's improvements since the Revolution are also far from unique. First, with respect to life expectancy, table 66 highlights that Cuba's absolute improvement of 16.0 years since the Revolution is surpassed by twenty-eight of the sixty-eight countries in our data set. Its percentage improvement of 25.7 percent is only thirty-second best. Regardless of which of the two measures of improvement one focuses on, Cuba's performance with respect to increasing life expectancy is by no means unique, despite all of the fanfare with respect to Cuba's supposed achievements in health care. Furthermore, while Cuban health care is free, Cuban medical facilities are greatly deteriorated, lack technology, and face vast shortages of the most basic medicines and medical supplies. The exception to this rule is that, in what amounts to an apartheid health care system, government elites and foreign medical tourists who can pay with hard currency have access to their own separate medical facilities that are well stocked and benefit from more advanced technologies and treatments.

The effect of Cuba's deteriorated socioeconomic condition has also manifested itself in a decreased desire for Cuban families to bare children. As a result, the Cuban population has aged significantly relative to where the country stood before the Revolution. The resulting markedly different population distribution, together with other factors such as suicides that have ballooned from six per one thousand deaths, at the onset of the Revolution, to eighty-three per one thousand deaths today—the second-highest suicide rate in the world—have led to Cuba going from having one of the lowest overall mortality rates in the world to now ranking in the bottom half of the countries in our data set. As table 67 highlights, of forty-six countries in our data set, Cuba's 36 percent increase in mortality is higher than that of all but three countries—Bulgaria, Iraq, and Russia.

Another statistic that the Castro government has often pointed to as a unique achievement has been infant mortality. While it is true that Cuba still ranks highly today with respect to this metric, it actually ranks below where it did in the 1950s relative to the other countries in our data set and thus no particularly exceptional achievement can truly be claimed. Whereas in the 1950s Cuba had a lower infant mortality rate than countries such as France, Germany, Italy, Spain, and Japan, all those countries have now surpassed Cuba in terms of their infant mortality indicators. In fact, as table 68 shows, Cuba's rate of reduction of infant mortality since the 1950s is only the twenty-first best out of the thirty-eight countries in our data set, and the absolute decline in infant mortality was bested by an even longer list of twenty-eight countries.

In addition to the detailed tables above, the summary comparisons below further underscore the extent of the deterioration in Cuba's socioeconomic standing after fifty-six years of Communism:

1. In 1959, there were 161 sugar mills in Cuba. Presently there are only 56, not all of which operate in any given year. According to the Oficina Nacional de Estadísticas de Cuba (Cuba's National Statistical Office) the island is now producing less sugar than it was a century ago, after having been the world's top sugar producer.

2. It has been remarkable how little the population has expanded in Cuba over more than fifty years. Many Latin American and Caribbean countries with roughly the same population as Cuba before the

Table 67. Mortality Rates per 1,000 Inhabitants in 2011.

#	Country	Mortality Rate Per 1,000 Inhabitants	Absolute Change	Absolute Change Rank	% Change	% Change Rank
1	Jordan	4.0	-4.3	10	-52%	7
2	Colombia	4.2	-9.1	2	-68%	1
4	Costa Rica	4.3	-5.3	6	-55%	4
3	Singapore	4.3	-3.2	13	-43%	11
5	Peru	4.5	-7.6	3	-63%	3
7	Venezuela	4.7	-5.3	7	-53%	6
6	Panama	4.7	-4.5	9	-49%	8
8	Ecuador	4.9	-9.9	1	-67%	2
9	Nicaragua	4.9	-3.2	14	-40%	12
10	Israel	5.2	-1.4	25	-21%	22
12	Iran	5.3	-2.4	20	-31%	15
11	Viet-Nam	5.3	-2.2	22	-29%	17
13	Philippines	5.5	-3.5	12	-39%	13
14	Iraq	5.5	1.7	38	45%	45
15	Chile	5.6	-6.5	4	-54%	5
16	Iceland	6	-1.2	26	-17%	26
17	Ireland	6.2	-5.5	5	-47%	9
20	China	6.5	-4.9	8	-43%	10
18	Australia	6.5	-2.6	17	-29%	18
21	Dominican Republic	6.5	-2.6	18	-29%	19
19	New Zealand	6.5	-2.5	19	-28%	20
22	Lebanon	6.7	1.2	37	22%	39
23	Bolivia	6.9	-3.1	15	-31%	16
24	Canada	7.1	-1.1	27	-13%	27
25	Argentina	7.8	-0.4	32	-5%	31
26	Netherlands	7.9	0.1	34	1%	34
27	**Cuba**	**7.9**	**2.1**	**43**	**36%**	**43**
28	Spain	8	-1.9	24	-19%	25

#	Country	Mortality Rate Per 1,000 Inhabitants	Absolute Change	Absolute Change Rank	% Change	% Change Rank
29	Switzerland	8.1	-2.1	23	-21%	23
30	Norway	8.1	-0.6	30	-7%	30
31	United States	8.3	-1.0	28	-11%	28
32	France	8.4	-4.1	11	-33%	14
33	Finland	8.9	-0.1	33	-1%	33
34	Sweden	9.2	-0.4	31	-4%	32
35	Greece	9.2	1.8	39	24%	41
36	Belgium	9.4	-2.8	16	-23%	21
37	Uruguay	9.4	2.4	44	34%	42
38	Italy	9.5	-0.8	29	-8%	29
39	Denmark	9.6	0.7	35	8%	35
40	Portugal	9.7	-2.4	21	-20%	24
41	Japan	9.8	1.8	41	23%	40
42	Poland	10	1.0	36	11%	36
43	Romania	11.7	1.8	40	18%	38
44	Hungary	12.4	1.9	42	18%	37
45	Bulgaria	13.6	4.2	45	45%	44
46	Russia	14.6	7.0	46	92%	46

Source: World Health Organization; Global Health Observatory Data Repository; Mortality and global health estimates: Crude birth and death rate Data by country; World Health Organization, 2011; Web; Dec. 2013.

    Revolution (such as Chile) now have 50 percent more inhabitants, and neighboring countries with much smaller land areas and lower populations before the Revolution now have nearly equivalent populations, such as the Dominican Republic and Haiti.

3.   Cuba had the lowest inflation in Latin America and the Caribbean in the late fifties and now arguably has one of the highest, once the lack of availability of goods and the black market prices are considered (United Nations Development Program, *Human Development Report*, 2010).

4.   The Cuban peso was at parity with the dollar in 1958, and presently it trades at around twenty-five Cuban pesos to the dollar. This is another way of measuring the extent to which sub rosa inflation has

Table 68. Infant Mortality Rates, 2005–2010.

#	Country	Infant Mortality Rate -per 1,000 Live Births	Absolute Change -per 1,000 Live Births	Absolute Change Rank	% Change	% Change Rank
1	Iceland	2.0	-21.7	36	-92%	14
2	Luxembourg	2.3	-43.4	27	-95%	6
3	Sweden	2.5	-20.8	38	-89%	16
4	Japan	2.6	-59.9	15	-96%	1
5	Finland	2.8	-45.5	26	-94%	7
6	Norway	3.0	-24.7	33	-89%	17
7	Italy	3.4	-70.5	13	-95%	3
8	Spain	3.6	-71.0	12	-95%	4
9	France	3.7	-56.5	16	-94%	8
10	Germany	3.7	-54.7	19	-94%	9
11	Ireland	3.7	-49.5	24	-93%	11
12	Austria	3.8	-71.4	10	-95%	5
13	Belgium	3.8	-53.4	22	-93%	10
14	Denmark	3.8	-30.7	30	-89%	18
15	Israel	3.9	-47.6	25	-92%	12
16	Netherlands	4.1	-22.7	35	-85%	24
17	Switzerland	4.2	-30.1	31	-88%	20
18	Australia	4.4	-20.9	37	-83%	28
19	United Kingdom	4.9	-29.2	32	-86%	23
20	**Cuba**	**5.1**	**-32.5**	**29**	**-86%**	**21**
21	Canada	5.2	-38.1	28	-88%	19
22	United States	6.9	-24.4	34	-78%	33
23	Puerto Rico	7.0	-71.3	11	-91%	15
24	Chile	7.2	-148.0	1	-95%	2
25	Costa Rica	9.9	-109.7	3	-92%	13
26	Thailand	11.8	-56.4	18	-83%	26
27	Argentina	13.4	-53.6	21	-80%	32
28	Mexico	16.7	-89.7	6	-84%	25
29	Venezuela	17.0	-73.7	8	-81%	30

#	Country	Infant Mortality Rate -per 1,000 Live Births	Absolute Change -per 1,000 Live Births	Absolute Change Rank	% Change	% Change Rank
30	Panama	17.1	-53.6	20	-76%	34
31	Colombia	19.1	-115.0	2	-86%	22
32	Peru	21.0	-84.2	7	-80%	31
33	Ecuador	21.1	-94.1	5	-82%	29
34	Nicaragua	21.5	-101.8	4	-83%	27
35	Suriname	22.2	-56.4	17	-72%	35
36	Honduras	27.8	-64.9	14	-70%	37
37	Dominican Republic	29.6	-51.7	23	-64%	38
38	Guatemala	30.1	-71.6	9	-70%	36

Source: United Nations, Department of Economic and Social Affairs, Population Division; World Population Prospects: The 2012 Revision; Infant mortality rate; United Nations Population Division, 2013; Web; Dec. 2013.

prevailed in Cuba over time (Oficina Nacional de Estadísticas de Cuba, *Anuario Estadístico*, 2013).

5. Calories per capita have also diminished, from 2,682 to 2,450, which is rare to see after more than fifty years of agricultural development in the world. Similarly, meat consumption per capita has plummeted from seventy-six to twelve pounds, and chicken consumption dropped from twelve to five pounds per inhabitant (Food and Agricultural Organization, *Annual Report*, 2014).

6. In the late fifties there used to be 6 million heads of cattle in Cuba. Now there are only 1.8 million. The number of heads of cattle per head of population as an index has plummeted from 1.00 to 0.16 per capita (Oficina Nacional de Estadísticas de Cuba, *Anuario Estadístico*, 2013).

7. Rice production has fallen from 611,000 metric tons to 369,000 metric tons per year.

8. With regard to incarceration, there were seven prisons in the pre-Castro era in Cuba. Now there are in the excess of 250 (United Nations Development Program, *Human Development Report*, 2010).

The number of prisoners has mushroomed from 6,000 to over 56,000, while the population of Cuba has slightly less than doubled (United Nations Development Program, *Human Development Report*, 2013). This, of course, has been one of the key ingredients in the Castro government's formula for maintaining itself in power for fifty six years.

Notes

1. Source: United Nations, United Nations Statistics Division; Industrial Commodity Statistics Database; World Comparison of the Number of Television Receivers Owned by the Citizens of the World; United Nations Statistics Division, 2010; Web; Dec. 2013. The population data utilized to convert total figures to per capita figures are from: United Nations, Department of Economic and Social Affairs, Population Division; World Population Prospects: The 2012 Revision; Total Population; United Nations Population Division, 2010; Web; Dec. 2013.

2. Source: World Bank (2013). "World Development Indicators 2013." Washington, D.C.: World Bank.

12

Conclusion

"Within twenty years at the most, he reflected, the huge and simple question, 'Was life better before the Revolution than it is now?' would have ceased once and for all to be answerable.... And when memory failed and written records were falsified—when that happened, the claim of the Party to have improved the conditions of human life had got to be accepted, because there did not exist, and never again could exist, any standard against which it could be tested."

When in the 1940s George Orwell penned the sentences above in his famous novel *Nineteen Eighty-Four*, few would have predicted that, just over a decade later, a communist dictatorship would take over Cuba and convert the country's reality into a mirror image of the horrors that Orwell imagined for his fictional world. Today, after more than fifty-six years under the Castro dictatorship, Cuba is in ruins. Incredibly, many throughout the world remain misinformed about the full depth of the damage caused by the Castro family's Communist dictatorship. Even more perplexing is how there are also those who, while informed, choose to distort Cuba's reality because accepting the clear failure of Cuba's Communist dictatorship demystifies ideals that they hold very dear.

In this book, we have provided a succinct overview of Cuba's developmental history. Through that overview, it is clear that Cuba's privileged historical position within the Spanish Empire and, particularly, its subsequent efforts as an independent republic between 1902 and 1959, led to developmental achievements before the Revolution that were nothing short of impressive. Fifty-six years after Communism took hold, however, the data we have presented speak volumes for how far Cuba has fallen.

While the Castro government has gone to great lengths to try to extoll Cuba's developmental record under Communism, this book clearly shows that, while most of the world has benefited from enormous economic development over the last fifty-six years, Cuba has overwhelmingly gone backward. In some cases, this has been true in an absolute sense, whereby important developmental indicators are, incredibly, actually lower today than they were fifty-six years ago. In other cases, Cuba's decline has been relative, whereby its progress has so significantly lagged behind the rest of the world that today it ranks among the least developed countries in the world—a far cry from the far more developed peer set it enjoyed before the Castro brothers usurped power.

The preceding chapters clearly show that before the Revolution of 1959, Cuba was socioeconomically ahead of a long list of countries, including a number of countries that today are among the most developed countries in the world. This was clear when, in chapter 2, we reviewed Cuba's rankings with respect to GDP per capita or when, in chapter 3, we examined the island's trade competitiveness, the strength of its foreign reserves, and the health of its monetary system.

Similarly, in terms of equality, while it is true that the economic conditions of all Cubans were not the same before 1959, it is also true that the level of inequality that existed was not materially different from that which existed in what today are considered developed economies. One can readily think, for example, of the difference in standards of living that existed across the different social classes and neighborhoods of large cities such as Madrid or New York City during the 1950s and how that inequality became even more pronounced when one compared income levels in those cities versus those seen in the small rural towns of their respective countries. The same was true in Cuba. There was inequality within Cuba's most developed city, Havana, and, in turn, Havana's socioeconomic development was greater than that of the island's countryside. However, there was nothing about the levels of inequality that existed in Cuba before the Revolution that was peculiar or particularly acute. In fact, the analysis we have presented in this book shows the opposite: that Cuba had better equality indicators in the 1950s than many of the most prosperous countries in the world. This was particularly clear when, in chapter 4, we presented Cuba's high rankings with respect to the percentage of GDP being paid as wages and, relatedly, showed that the entire island's consumption levels, both of basic items such as proteins and other foodstuffs, as well as items that would require high levels of discretionary income, such as radios, televisions, and automobiles, were sufficiently broad so as to place Cuba ahead of a number of developed nations. Chapter 5 showed that Cuba's economic successes also translated into it being able to make significant investments in education and health care. This resulted in Cubans having high (for the times) literacy rates and participation levels in higher education and some of the lowest rates of infant and overall mortality in the world.

Last, as the decade of the 1950s came to a close, Cuba was well poised for further economic advancement. Chapter 6 demonstrated that the island's economy was well into a stage of developmental take-off that could have provided for years of sustained and strong growth that could have led to Cuba's economic indicators reaching developed nation status.

Over the years, academics and commentators on Cuban history have argued that lack of economic development and inequality catalyzed the uprising of a discontented proletariat in the form of the Cuban Revolution. This book makes clear that this portrayal is not accurate. What Cuba's history proves is, in fact, the opposite. Namely, it demonstrates that, *in spite of economic development*, political instability combined with weak governmental and non-governmental institutions can suffice to bring about swift and radical changes that can shackle a country with decades of totalitarian rule.

As chapters 7 to 11 describe, what has transpired in Cuba after the Revolution amounts to nothing short of an economic catastrophe. The nationalization of the country's entire productive capacity by the Castro government made enemies of those who had invested in the island, both foreign and domestic, and of those whose entrepreneurial drive had created the businesses that provided the ample goods and services that the Cuban population enjoyed and the jobs that allowed Cubans to be productive members of society. With those who had driven economic activity on the island finding themselves either marginalized within Cuba or driven to exile, the country's competitiveness vis-à-vis foreign trading partners withered away, and its ability to sustain itself domestically decayed to the point that Cuba today is one of the poorest and most dysfunctional economies in the world.

Within this dysfunction a sharp inequality also exists among Cuban society between the standards of living of government elites and the rest of the Cuban population. Government elites, on the one hand, live relatively well. They enjoy access to the better homes on the island (usually confiscated from their previous owners), own cars (which are generally poor by world standards, but which provide for private transport, a coveted luxury on the island), and have access to a far broader set of goods and services than the rest of the population.

Most Cubans, on the other hand, regardless of years of study, ambition, or work ethic, must accept a life plagued by the daily shortage of even the most basic necessities and must endure the desperation of being trapped in a system that does not provide the slightest opportunity for personal advancement. All of that, of course, is accompanied by an omnipresent government that, through its many repressive agencies and tactics, relentlessly works to ensure that Cubans do not dare to attempt to effectuate the changes in government that they would surely seek if the repercussions were not beatings, jail terms, exile, and, in many cases, death.

Despite Cuba's calamitous experience over the last fifty-six years and the staying power (by force) of the Castro brothers' ruinous government, history shows that, sooner or later, repressive governments are eventually ousted and replaced by more open societies. When Cuba finally takes the steps to re-establish democracy and a free-market economy, Cubans will need to make important decisions with respect to how to reform Cuban society based on a clearheaded review of what has and has not worked in the past. Similarly, global capital markets will have to make determinations as to whether or not to allocate the billions of dollars of capital necessary to rebuild Cuba. When those determinations are being made, this book can provide a useful, succinct benchmark of the level of developmental success that the Cuban work ethic and entrepreneurial spirit can generate in a free society. It is indisputable that, as noted Cambridge University developmental economist Peter Bauer discusses in *Reality and Rhetoric*, a society's ambition and idiosyncrasies with respect to entrepreneurialism and development are key drivers of the success of any nation and the possibilities that it has to revive itself after a period of economic or political shock. The developmental success that Cuba experienced during its Republican period between 1902 and 1959, as well as the tremendous economic success achieved by Cuban exiles in the United States and elsewhere where they have been able to participate in free-market based economies bode well for Cuba's future. Once Cuba is able to rejoin the free world and succeeds at establishing a strong institutional framework that upholds the rule of law and protects private property, it is a good bet that the largest of the Antilles will experience the sort of economic rebirth about which many future case studies and books shall be written.

Bibliography

Alvarez, Jose and Lazaro Peña Castellanos. *Cuba's Sugar Industry*. University Press of Florida, Gainesville, Florida, 2001

American Chamber of Commerce of Cuba. *Cuba: Facts and Figures*. Havana: American Chamber of Commerce of Cuba, 1955.

Banco de Fomento Agrícola e Industrial de Cuba. *Anuario 1955*. Havana: BANFAIC, 1955.

Banco Nacional de Cuba. *Memoria 1954–55*. Havana: Banco Nacional de Cuba, 1954.

Banco Nacional de Cuba. *Memoria 1958–59*. Havana: Banco Nacional de Cuba, 1959.

Banco Nacional de Cuba. *Revista del Banco Nacional*. Havana: Banco Nacional de Cuba, May, 1959.

Bauer, Peter T., and Basil S. Yamey. *The Economics of Underdeveloped Countries*. Chicago: University of Chicago Press, 1957.

Bauer, Peter T. *Reality and Rhetoric: Studies in the Economics of Development*. Cambridge, Massachusetts: Harvard University Press, 1984.

Caribbean Journal Staff. "Cuba Reports Record Number of Tourist Arrivals in 2012." *The Caribbean Journal*. 11 January 2013. Web. July 2014.

Castrocare in Crisis. Foreign Affairs. N.p., 1 Mar. 2015. Web. 1 Mar. 2015.

Central Intelligence Agency. *Cuba: Handbook of Trade Statistics*, 1996, Langley, Virginia, USA, 1996.

Central Intelligence Agency. *Cuba: Handbook of Trade Statistics*, 2000, Langley, Virginia, USA, 2000.

Central Intelligence Agency. *The World Factbook; Literacy*, 2013; Web; Dec. 2013.

Clark, Colin. *Conditions of Economic Progress*. London: MacMillan, 1957.

Collegium of Cuban Economists. *The Cuban Economy Past, Present and Future*. Ed. Antonio Jorge and Jorge Salazar-Carrillo. Coral Gables: Collegium of Cuban Economists, 1997.

Commission on Cuban Affairs. *Problems of the New Cuba*. New York: Foreign Policy Association, 1935.

Cordero, Manuel, *Trabajadores*. July 8, 2002.

Cordova, Efren. "La Nueva Tarifa General de Salarios Minimos de Cuba." *Revista Cubana de Derecho*. 30.2 (1958).

Cuba in Transition, Volume 2, Association for the Study of the Cuban Economy, Washington, DC, 1992, pg. 126.

Cuba in Transition, Volume 3, Association for the Study of the Cuban Economy, Washington, DC, 1993, pg. 295.

Cuban Banking Study Group. *Cuba: Past, Present, and Future of its Banking and Financial System*. Miami: Cuban Banking Study Group, 1995.

Cuban Constitution. Article LXI, 1940.

Cuban Economic Research Project. *Stages and Problems of Industrial Development in Cuba*. Coral Gables: University of Miami Press, 1965.

Cuban Economic Research Project, University of Miami. *A Study on Cuba*. Coral Gables: University of Miami Press, 1965.

Cuban Economic Research Project, University of Miami. *Labor Conditions in Communist Cuba*. Coral Gables: University of Miami Press, 1963.

Cuban Economic Research Project, University of Miami. *Sugar in Cuba*. Coral Gables: University of Miami Press, 1966.

F. O. Licht, "International Sugar and Sweetener Report," 130, 14 (29 April 1998), pgs. 221–224.

Freyre, Jorge F. "The Cuban Economy in the Decade of 1948–1958." *The Cuban Economy: Past, Present and Future*. Ed. Antontio Jorge and Jorge Salazar-Carrillo. Coral Gables: Collegium of Cuban Economists, 1997.

Gonzalez, Edward. "Castro and Cuba's New Orthodoxy." *Problems of Communism*. 25 (1976).

Harbron, John D. *Trafalgar and the Spanish Navy*. London: Conway Maritime Press, 1988.

Historic Consumer Price Index 1800–1998. Ann Arbor: University of Michigan Documents Center, 2003.

Horowitz, Irving Louis, *The Conscience of Worms and the Cowardice of Lions: Cuban Politics and Culture in an American Context*, Miami: University of Miami North/South Center & Transaction Publishers, 1993, 81 pp.

Illan, Jose M. *Cuba: Facts and Figures of an Economy in Ruins*. Trans. George A. Wehby. Miami: Editorial ATP, 1964.

International Labour Organization; ILOSTAT; World Comparison of the Percentage of GDP paid as Compensation to Employees; International Labour Organization, 2008; Web; Dec. 2013.

International Labour Organization (ILO). *Statistical Supplement July 1959*. Geneva: International Labor Organization, 1959.

International Labour Organization (ILO). *Yearbook of Labour Statistics 1962*. Geneva: International Labor Organization, 1962.

International Monetary Fund, Direction of Trade Statistics Yearbook, Washington, DC, 2003.

International Road Federation; World Road Statistics and data files; World Comparison of Inhabitants per Passenger Vehicle; World Bank, 2008; Web; Dec. 2013.

International Sugar Organization, Sugar Year Book, London, 1989–2002.

International Telecommunication Union, Telecommunication Development Bureau, ICT Data and Statistics Division; World Telecommunication/ICT Indicators Database; Fixed-telephone subscriptions; Telecommunication Development Bureau, 2013; Web; Dec. 2013.

International Telecommunication Union, Telecommunication Development Bureau, ICT Data and Statistics Division; World Telecommunication/ICT Indicators Database; Mobile-cellular subscriptions; Telecommunication Development Bureau, 2013; Web; Dec. 2013.

International Telecommunication Union, Telecommunication Development Bureau, ICT Data and Statistics Division; World Telecommunication/ICT Indicators Database; Percentage of individuals using the Internet; Telecommunication Development Bureau, 2013; Web; Dec. 2013.

Jorge, Antonio. "Ideology, Planning, Efficiency, and Growth: Change Without Development." *Cuban Communism*. 6th ed. Ed. Irving Louis Horowitz. New Brunswick: Transaction Books, 1987.

Kravis, Irving, Alan Heston and Robert Summers. *World Product and Income: International Comparisons of Real Gross Product*. Baltimore: Johns Hopkins University Press, 1982.

Luna, Félix. *Breve Historia de los Argentinos*. Buenos Aires: Grupo Editorial Planeta, 2000.

Mestre, Jose A. *The Cuba Castro-Communism Destroyed*. Coral Gables: University of Miami Press, 1961.

Morales, Emilio and Scarpaci, Joseph L. "Remittances Drive the Cuban Economy." The Havana Consulting Group. 11 June 2013. Web. 7 July 2014

Oficina Nacional De Estadística E Información, República de Cuba. "Work Force and Salaries." Anuario Estadístico de Cuba 2011. Edición 2012

Orwell, George. *Nineteen Eighty-Four*. New York: Penguin Group, 2003.

Oshima, Harry T. "A New Estimate of the National Income and Product of Cuba in 1953." *Food Research Institute Studies*. Palo Alto: Stanford University Food Research Institute, Nov. 1961.

Panamerican Union. *América en Cifras 1960*. Washington, DC: Panamerican Union, 1960.

Pazos, Felipe. *Medio Siglo de Política Económica Latinoamericana*. Caracas: Academia Nacional de Ciencias Económicas, 1992.

Perez-Lopez, Jorge F. *An Index of Cuban Industrial Output 1930–1958*. Diss SUNY Albany, 1974. Ann Arbor: University of Michigan, 1995. Microfilm.

Perez-Lopez, Jorge F. and Jose Alvarez, *Reinventing the Cuban Sugar Agroindustry*, Lexington Books, 2005.

Perez-Lopez, Jorge F., *The Economics of Cuban Sugar*, University of Pittsburg Press, Pittsburgh, Pennsylvania, 1991.

Pick Publishing Corporation. *Pick's Currency Yearbook 1957*. New York: Pick Publishing Corporation, 1957.

Pick Publishing Corporation. *Pick's Currency Yearbook 1959*. New York: Pick Publishing Corporation, 1959.

Portuondo, Fernando. *Cuba Republicana: Las Paginas que Prohibió Fidel Castro*. San Juan: Ediciones Capiro, 1985.

Rajan, Raghuram G. and Zingales, Luigi. "The Great Reversals: The Politics of Financial Development in the 20th. Century". *Journal of Financial Economics* 69 (2003) 5–50.

Ritter, Archibald, ed., *The Cuban Economy*, University of Pittsburgh Press, 2004.

Rostow, Walt W. *The Process of Economic Growth*. New York: Norton, 1962.

Rostow, Walt W. *The Stages of Economic Growth: A Non-Communist Manifesto*. Cambridge: Cambridge University Press, 1961.

Salazar-Carrillo, Jorge and Antonio Jorge, eds., *The Economics of the Caribbean Basin: Present Problems and Future Trends*, University of Stockholm, 1997.

Salazar-Carrillo, Jorge and Antonio Jorge. *The Future of the Cuban Economy*. University of Miami, Coral Gables: Collegium of Cuban Economists, 2004.

Salazar-Carrillo, Jorge, "Independence and Economic Performance in Cuba" in Irving Louis Horowitz, editor, *Cuban Communism*, 7th Ed. New Brunswick, New Jersey: Transaction Publishers, 1989.

Salazar-Carrillo, Jorge, *Oil in the Economic Development of Venezuela*, Praeger Publishers, New York, 1976.

Salazar-Carrillo, Jorge. "One Hundred Years of Cuban Economy." *Herencia*. 8.1–2.

Salazar-Carrillo, Jorge, "Primary Type Export Activities as Leading Sectors in Economic Development," University Microfilms, Ann Arbor, Michigan, 1967.

Salazar-Carrillo, Jorge. "The National Economic Accounting System of Cuba." Ed. Irving Louis Horowitz. *Cuban Communism*. 6th Ed. New Brunswick, New Jersey: Transaction, 1987.

Salazar-Carrillo, Jorge. "The Cuban Economy as Seen Through Its Trading Partners." Ed. Irving Louis Horowitz. *Cuban Communism*. 9th Ed. New Brunswick, New Jersey: Transaction Publishers, 1998.

Salazar-Carrillo, Jorge. and D.S. Prasada-Rao, eds. *World Comparisons of Incomes, Prices and Product*. New York: North Holland-Elsevier, 1988.

Social Security Administration; Measures Of Central Tendency for Wage Data; Average and Median Amounts of Net Compensation; Social Security Administration, 2012; Web; Dec. 2013.

Statistical Office of the United Nations, Department of Economic and Social Affairs. *Monthly Bulletin of Statistics*. New York: Statistical Office of the United Nations, November, 1957.

Statistical Office of the United Nations, Department of Economic and Social Affairs. *Demographic Yearbook 1955*. New York: Statistical Office of the United Nations, 1955.

Statistical Office of the United Nations, Department of Economic and Social Affairs. *Demographic Yearbook 1958*. New York: Statistical Office of the United Nations, 1958.

Statistical Office of the United Nations, Department of Economic and Social Affairs. *Demographic Yearbook 1961*. New York: Statistical Office of the United Nations, 1961.

Statistical Office of the United Nations, Department of Economic and Social Affairs. *Monthly Bulletin of Statistics*. New York: Statistical Office of the United Nations, 1960.

Statistical Office of the United Nations, Department of Economic and Social Affairs. *Monthly Bulletin of Statistics*. New York: Statistical Office of the United Nations, 1961.

Statistical Office of the United Nations, Department of Economic and Social Affairs. *Statistical Yearbook 1957*. New York: Statistical Office of the United Nations, 1957.

Statistical Office of the United Nations, Department of Economic and Social Affairs. *Statistical Yearbook 1958*. New York: Statistical Office of the United Nations, 1958.

Statistical Office of the United Nations, Department of Economic and Social Affairs. *Statistical Yearbook 1959*. New York: Statistical Office of the United Nations, 1959.

Statistical Office of the United Nations, Department of Economic and Social Affairs. *Statistical Yearbook 1960*. New York: Statistical Office of the United Nations, 1960.

Statistical Office of the United Nations, Department of Economic and Social Affairs. *Statistical Yearbook 1960*. New York: Statistical Office of the United Nations, 1960. Pg. 600.

Statistical Office of the United Nations, Department of Economic and Social Affairs. *Statistical Yearbook 1961*. New York: Statistical Office of the United Nations, 1961.

Statistical Office of the United Nations, Department of Economic and Social Affairs. *Statistical Yearbook 1962*. New York: Statistical Office of the United Nations, 1962.

Statistical Office of the United Nations, Department of Economic and Social Affairs. *Demographic Yearbook 1960*. New York: Statistical Office of the United Nations, 1960.

Statistical Office of the United Nations. *National and Per Capita Income in 70 Countries*. New York: Statistical Office of the United Nations, 1950.

Svejnar, Jan, "Transition Economies: Performance and Challenges," *Journal of Economic Perspectives*, Vol. 16, Number 1, 2002.

Thomas, Hugh. *Cuba: The Pursuit of Freedom*. New York: Harper & Row, 1971.

Tone, John Lawrence. *War and Genocide in Cuba, 1895–1898*. Chapel Hill: University of North Carolina Press, 2006.

UNESCO. *Annuaire International De L'éducation*. Paris: UNESCO, 1959.

UNESCO Institute for Statistics; UIS Data Centre; Daily newspapers: Total average circulation per 1,000 inhabitants; UNESCO, 2004; Web; Dec. 2013.

United Nations Commission for Latin America and the Caribbean, (ECLAC), *La Economia Cubana*. Fondo de Cultura Economica, Mexico D.F., 2000, pg. 515.

United Nations Economic Commission for Latin America and the Caribbean (ECLAC), *The Cuban Economy. Structural Reforms and Economic Performance in 1990s*, LC/MEX/R.746/Rev. 1, 6 December, 2001.

United Nations Statistics Division; Millennium Development Goals Database; Literacy Rate; United Nations Statistics Division, 2011; Web; Dec. 2013.

United Nations Statistics Division; National Accounts Estimates of Main Aggregates; United Nations Statistics Division, 2011; Web; Dec. 2013.

United Nations, Department of Economic and Social Affairs, Population Division; World Population Prospects: The 2012 Revision; Infant mortality rate; United Nations Population Division, 2013; Web; Dec. 2013.

United Nations, Department of Economic and Social Affairs, Population Division; World Population Prospects: The 2012 Revision; Life Expectancy at Birth; United Nations Population Division, 2012; Web; Dec. 2013.

United Nations, Department of Economic and Social Affairs, Population Division; World Population Prospects: The 2012 Revision; Life Expectancy at Birth; United Nations Population Division, 2012; Web; Mar. 2014.

United Nations, Department of Economic and Social Affairs, Population Division; World Population Prospects: The 2012 Revision; Total Population; United Nations Population Division, 2010; Web; Dec. 2013.

United Nations, Economic Commission for Latin America (CEPAL). *Economic Survey of Latin America 1957*. New York: United Nations Department of Economic and Social Affairs, 1959.

United Nations, Educational, Scientific and Cultural Organization (UNESCO). *Statistical Yearbook 1963*. Paris: UNESCO, 1963.

United Nations, Food and Agriculture Organization (FAO). *Monthly Bulletin of Agricultural and Economic Statistics*. 7 (1958).

United Nations, United Nations Statistics Division; Industrial Commodity Statistics Database; World Comparison of the Number of Television Receivers Owned by the Citizens of the World; United Nations Statistics Division, 2010; Web; Dec. 2013.

United States Bureau of the Census. *Statistical Abstract of the United States 1959*. Ed. 81. Washington, DC: United States Department of Commerce, 1959.

United States Bureau of the Census. *Statistical Abstract of the United States 1960*. Ed. 81. Washington, DC: United States Department of Commerce, 1960.

United States Census Bureau. "Trade in Goods with Cuba." U.S. International Trade Data 2014. Web. July 2014

United States Department of Commerce. *Investment in Cuba: Basic Information for United States Businessmen*. Washington, DC: US Government Printing Office, 1956.

Wall Street Journal, November 12, 2003.

Wallich, Henry C. *Monetary Problems of an Export Economy: The Cuban Experience 1914–1947*. Cambridge: Harvard University Press, 1950.

World Bank. *World Development Indicators 2013*. Washington, D.C.: World Bank. Web; Oct 2013.

World Health Organization; Global Health Observatory Data Repository; Mortality and global health estimates: Crude birth and death rate Data by country; World Health Organization, 2011; Web; Dec. 2013.

Yearbook, Vol. II.; Total Trade; United Nations Statistics Division, 2008–2012; Web; Dec. 2013. Latest available trade data for Cuba is from 2008. The population figures utilized in order to arrive at per capita values are from United Nations, Department of Economic and Social Affairs, Population Division; World Population Prospects: The 2012 Revision; Total Population; United Nations Population Division, 2010; Web; Dec. 2013.

Zúñiga, Antonio Ramos. "The Royal Dockyard of Havana." *Herencia*.15.3 (2009).

About the Authors

Jorge Salazar-Carrillo is a Cuban American who simultaneously studied law at the University of Habana and economics at the University of Villanova at Habana. He obtained his bachelor of business administration at the University of Miami in 1958. In 1959 he was named director of the Economics Group at the Finance Ministry in Cuba, the youngest director ever in the history of the country. After being awarded United Nations, British Council, and Organization of American States awards and fellowships, he obtained his master's degree and PhD in economics from the University of California (Berkeley). He was awarded a Brookings Institution Research Fellowship, and later became a senior fellow (the youngest ever) at that institution. Concurrently, he was professorial lecturer at Georgetown University and research associate at the Wharton School of Economics of the University of Pennsylvania. On leave from Brookings he became a director of a United Nations program in Brazil. In 1979 the Department of Economics of Florida International University brought him as chairman of the Department of Economics to establish the master's degree and PhD in Economics, while remaining a Brookings Fellow. He has published eighty-three books and hundreds of articles and essays. He has taught in China, Brazil, Mexico, Holland, Central America, and Venezuela.

Andro Nodarse-León was born in Havana, Cuba, and lived in there until the age of eleven. He migrated to Madrid, Spain, in 1988 and came to Miami, Florida, in 1989. Mr. Nodarse-León attended the University of Pennsylvania, where he graduated with honors, receiving a bachelor of science in economics from the Wharton School and a bachelor of science in systems engineering from the School of Engineering and Applied Sciences. He began his career in New York City as an investment banker at Goldman, Sachs & Co., where he advised a number of large-cap telecommunications, media, and entertainment businesses with respect to mergers, acquisitions, strategic and financing matters. After Goldman Sachs, Mr. Nodarse-León worked as a private equity

181

investment executive at Kohlberg, Kravis, Roberts & Co. (KKR) in New York City. At KKR, Mr. Nodarse-León focused on the acquisition of businesses in the consumer products, media, entertainment, and hospitality industries. In 2005, Mr. Nodarse-León co-founded LEÓN, MAYER & Co., (LM) a private equity and investment banking firm based in Miami and New York City. Mr. Nodarse-León is the co-chair of the Board of Directors of Endeavor Schools, a leading pre-K to 12th grade private school business founded and owned by LEÓN, MAYER & Co. He serves as a vice-president of the Board of Directors of the Cuban American National Foundation, is the Chair of the Governance Committee of the Board of Directors of the Foundation for Human Rights in Cuba and previously served as Trustee for the Oliver Scholars Program in New York City.

Index